THERE IS HOPE FOR BLACKS & WHITES

by

Rev. Douglas Ahamefula

RoseDog Books
PITTSBURGH, PENNSYLVANIA 15238

RoseDog Books
585 Alpha Drive
Suite 103
Pittsburgh, PA 15238
Visit our website at *www.rosedogbookstore.com*

ISBN: 978-1-64957-937-9
eISBN: 978-1-64957-958-4

Contents

FOREWORD

This book is written to tell both Black and white people in America and in all over the world that there is HOPE. A nation like America has continued to experience protests upon protests caused by social injustice in the society but there is light at the end of the channel. Martin Luther King Jr., the human rights activist, once said that he had a dream. Some dreams take a while to be realized but wait until the dream is realized. I have divided this book into PART "A" and PART "B."

PART "A" (Chapters 1-3) of this book is about the root of the social injustice that now is existing in our society and evidence of HOPE that would soon be realized.

PART "B" (Chapters 4-8) of this book is the collections of Bible-based inspirational writings and Biblical teachings shared with me by a dear friend, Rev. Dr. Paul Fakunle, of God's Family Church.

PART "C" (Chapters 9-13) of this book are my personal gospel messages and are intended to bring Hope in God through our Lord Jesus Christ, to the reader.

It is my sincere prayer and desire that by the time you finish reading this book, HOPE will resonate in the reader's heart.

⟫⟪

Chapter 1

HOPE AFTER THE DEATH OF GEORGE FLOYD

The events and protests all over the world that followed the killing of a Black man known as George Floyd, on May 25, 2020, in a Minneapolis neighborhood, under the watchful eyes of other three white police officers, is a sign that there is Hope for Black and white people in America. It is a dawn of a new day to see both black and white coming out in mass to protest against social injustice in the American society. It was at the peak of the Covid-19 deadly pandemic that has already claimed the lives of over two hundred thousand lives in America. Both black and white people did not mind but came out in mass to protest against the social injustice in the land. In many towns across the world, they were white protesters more than black protesters. The racial injustice in our society and the worldwide protest that preceded the killing of the black man, George Floyd, is rooted in the collective memory of its people and its past. However, for generations we have failed to recognize the cause of the deepest wounds in our nation's history. Our black, indigenous people and people of color have suffered through slavery and genocide for hundreds of years followed by decades of segregation and systematic oppression. With the increase of more white folks, especially the white youth, waking up to join the protest of "Black Lives Matter," it can be said that we are living in an incredible moment in history. We are now presented with the opportunity for real, structural change that we simply cannot ignore. It has been said and written that there is a time for everything under the sun. A time to be born and a time to die. A time to hate, and a time to love. A time to plant seeds and a time to harvest the fruits of the seeds that were planted. A time to enslave others and a time to set the slaves free. A time of social injustice, and a time of social reconciliation. The significance of more white people than black protesters in many towns, following the killing of a black man by a white police officer, shows that more white people are now waking up to stop this evil social injustice against black people. It is sad that many people adopted racism as a way of life following the abolition of slavery and are guilty of this evil. Some school of thoughts have said that we need to wait for these racist generations for all to die away before we can have social reconciliation.

The white police officer who had his knee on the neck of the black man, George Floyd, had no intention to allow him to continue to stay alive. Even when George complained that he could not breathe, the white police officer still continued to pin down his knee on his neck. The black protesters were indirectly saying to all the racists, "You have your knees on our necks for too long, you see, we cannot breathe. Take away your knees away from our necks so we can breathe." The blacks are not asking for something too difficult to grant. They are simply asking to be treated like every other people. They are simply saying that if you keep having your knees on our necks for a long period of time, we may eventually die for lack of oxygen. That was exactly what killed George Floyd. No human being can live without oxygen for a very long period of time.

Some of these racially and socially biased individuals even speak against people protesting against social injustice. They are against the slogan "Black Lives Matter." When it is said, "Black Lives Matter," it means to say "As White Lives Matter so Do Black Lives Matter." The younger generation of white people are now are taking sides with their black counterparts to question their older folks why Black people should be treated differently. They are saying by joining the protest of "Black Lives Matter" that this evil practice of unfair social injustice has to end. This is in agreement with Thomas Jefferson's penned statement in 1776, that "All men are created equal." It was slavery that gave birth to racism. The origin of racism can be traced back to the era when black people were forcefully kidnapped from Africa and brought to America in chains and sold as slaves in American slave markets to serve in the sugarcane plantations and in the white American homes. If there is anyone to blame for this dreadful act, it would be those American forefathers who indulged in slavery and not the descendants of those slaves who inherited the unjustified social injustice. These slaves were treated as subhuman beings and after the abolition of slavery, the freed slaves were still deprived of their basic rights such as voting rights, use of public facilities, freedom to live anywhere they wanted, and so on.

As time goes on many of these rights were given back to the descendants of the free slaves but the issue of social justice and discrimination still remains. It must be noted that the enslavement of black people from Africa differs from the practice of slavery in the Biblical period. Then, black people were forcefully kidnapped from their homeland in Africa and brought to America in chains. During the Biblical period a man could voluntary give himself or any member of his family to another wealthy man as a slave. This could be because of economic reasons. A man might owe another man a debt he could not pay;

in exchange to settle his debts, he might then give any of his sons or daughters to his debtor as a settlement. Sometimes there would be a war between two nations; the winner would then take the people of the nation that was defeated as slaves.

PART "A"

CHAPTER 2

THE EVIL THAT COMES FROM RACISM

The famous American preacher the late Billy Graham once said that Sundays are the most freely divided day in America. On Sundays, many white churches would not welcome black people into their churches. A black person who visits a white church on Sunday but noticed that he was not well received would not want to go back to that white church. Hardly would you find a white person attending a black church no matter how good the preacher can be in that black church. Black people would not mind attending a white church provided they are received in that white church. This ought not to be so. God created both white and black people. It shows that God the creator loves varieties; he loves white, black, brown, or any other color you may find. He made some fat, some slim, some tall, and some short. Heaven and hell would be filled with people of different colors and sizes. You better choose to live with any other colors of human beings on earth because you can never avoid them. The early church of Jesus Christ was very conscious about the racial issues in the church, especially between the Jewish converts and the Greek converts. As soon as they noticed it, they took action to make sure that everyone was treated fairly. It was for this reason the man Stephen was appointed to handle the issue in Acts 6:5. If you are a white pastor, pastoring a church in an area filled with people from a different race but your church is only filled with white folks, then you must know that you are doing something wrong. It may be that your ministry is still based on racial bias. The killing of the black man, George Floyd, by a white police officer prompted day protests all over the world. Some criminals snuck in among the protesters, took the advantage to loot goods from a few stores in cities like California and New York. Other took the advantage to pull down statues erected in honor of some known slave masters. Some that are racially biased have capitalized on the protesters' actions. They never condemned the racially motivated killing of the black man, George Floyd, but are more concerned about the lootings by a few criminals and the pulling down of statues of slave masters. Those statues shouldn't have been erected in the first place because of their evil action in the slave trade. In Exodus 20:4, God forbids his children from erecting statues or images of anything or anyone to place it in a place for everyone to see. By have the statues of those slaves' masters and placing them in public places, it is a direct disobedience to God's commandment. The purpose of having those statues is an indirect way of giving the glory that rightfully belongs to God to the slave masters, who were represented in those statues. Look at what is written in Isaiah 42:8: "I am the Lord, that is My name; And My glory I will not give to another, nor My praise to carved images."

CHAPTER 3

NONCHALANT ATTITUDE TOWARDS RACISM

The reason why racism still exists today is because many people have chosen not to speak out against it. Even many white Christians are guilty for the reason of their silence. You would expect that the white Church would stand up to condemn the evil practices of racism and social injustice but they would not even talk about it or even lead a protest against it. It is just like being in a Democrat party or Republic party in America. When Christian Democrats hear their leader promoting abortion rights and gay rights issues, he or she would bury her or his head in the sand pretending not to hear it. When a Christian Republican hears their leader making dehumanizing statements against women, and black people, saying that it is only a bathroom talk, he or she would bury his or her head in the sand pretending not to hear it. There may be reasons why God allowed all these protests, looting and unrest in our land. It can be summed up by saying that God did not approve the racism and the social injustice in the land. In the book of

Proverbs 16:7, it reads: "When a man's way pleases the Lord, he makes his enemies to be at peace with him." It is likely because the ways of our society are not pleasing to God. When the black man, George Floyd, was killed by a white police officer, many people, both whites and blacks, protested over his racially motivated killing by a white police officer. 99% of all the protesters did not know George Floyd personally.

I can still remember what Hanaah Sfameni said during her graduation celebration before the death of George Floyd. Hanaah is the daughter of a prominent Assembly of God Church Pastor. Hanaah is in her early twenties and graduated from a law school. In her remarks during her graduation celebration from law school, she said that she chose to study law because she found lots of injustice in our society. She said that she has studied law because she wants to be a voice to some of those who have been suffering injustice.

During the time when a white officer pinned his knee on the neck of the black man, George Floyd, there were three other white police officers standing by. By their nonchalant attitude towards the dying black man, they were showing sign of approval over the action of the fellow white police officer who had his knee on the neck of the black man, George Floyd. People took this opportunity to protest, demanding change in our social justice and end to racism. The black people who were protesting were motivated from the fact that they have experienced a non-ending mistreatment from many white folks because of the color of their black skin. They are indirectly saying, "Please, stop maltreating us, stop discriminating against us and stop killing us because just as the Lives of white people matter to you, so the Lives of black people matter to us." The white people who joined the protest did so because they have for a long time been eyewitnesses to the ill treatment of black people because of the color of their skin. Every animal always sticks to its kind and would be ready to defend its kind when possible. The animals do not judge or discriminate over the skin color of the animals of the same species. Man, who is supposed to be more intelligent and should know better, has chosen to enslave and discriminate against its own kind. If you are a white or black person and still discriminate against people of other race, then know for sure that something is wrong with your thoughts. Know for sure that the new generation is here. The world is no longer ready to wait until you correct your wrong thoughts of overdue racial discrimination but would march forward towards racial reconciliation. There is hope for Black and white people in America.

Part "B"

✦

Chapter 4

A. NO PROBLEM IS TOO BIG FOR GOD

Matthew 14:30: "But when he saw the wind boisterous, he was afraid; and beginning to sink, he cried, saying, Lord, save me." Peter couldn't have walked on the water apart from Jesus even if it had been calm. The circumstances simply took Peter's attention off of his Master and led him back into carnal thinking. Likewise, Satan tries to distract us by thinking about our problems.

Peter's faith didn't fail him all at once, as can be seen, that he only "began" to sink. If there had been no faith present, he would have sunk all at once and not gradually. This illustrates that the entrance of fear and the exit of faith does not happen instantly. There are always signs that this is happening. If we will turn our attention back to Jesus, as Peter did, He will save us from drowning. No problem is too big for God. We should cast our care about the problem over on God and just keep our eyes on Jesus, the Word.

B. OUR BATTLE AGAINST THE DEVIL

"Casting down imaginations, and every high thing that exalted itself against the knowledge of God, and bringing into captivity every thought to the obedience of Christ" (2 Corinthians 10:5, KJV). "We demolish arguments and every pretension that sets itself up against the knowledge of God, and we take captive every thought to make it obedient to Christ" (2 Corinthians 10:5, NIV).

Both of these areas deal with the mind. Our battle against the devil takes place right between our ears. The mind is the battlefield in which thoughts and reasoning contrary to God's Word are to be captured and submitted to Christ, our Commander. Just as enemy soldiers are captured in war, so rebel thoughts must be taken captive and made to submit to Christ.

This is an amazing statement! Paul was saying that it is not only possible to take every thought captive, but that our spiritual weapons were designed for the express purpose of taking every thought captive and making them obedient to Christ. Keeping our minds completely stayed upon the Lord is an obtainable goal. It doesn't matter what you are facing today... no problem is too big when you factor in God's power! Take hold of His power by expecting something good to happen to you.

C. NO MATTER WHAT SATAN THROWS AGAINST US

When you accepted Jesus as your Lord, He took your name. Your name was sin. Your name was weakness. Your life was ruled by fear, and hell was your destination. Then you accepted Jesus. He gave Himself to you. You gave yourself to Him. His life became yours. Your life became His. You turned loose of natural man as your father and received God as your Father. Ephesians 3:15 says the Church has been named after Him—that's you and me!

If we want to receive God's blessings, it is important that we stay in contact with other believers in the body of Christ. Those who isolate themselves from God's family and try to go it alone cut themselves off from God's power (Philippians 2:9). When poverty calls, don't answer yes. Say no! When your body calls itself sick, say, "No! That's not my name. I am healed." When Satan tries to tell you you're alone and discouraged, answer him out loud, "That's not in my covenant. I am loved and strong in the Lord." No matter what Satan tries to throw against you, the Name of the Lord is stronger. Whatever the Lord has called Himself in His Word is who you are now!

D. CONFESSING WHAT WE BELIEVE

To maintain our victory over Satan, we must speak forth the Word of God, which is the sword of the Spirit (Ephesians 6:17). In our English translations, two different words are used for the "Word" of God. The most common is "logos" and it indicates the whole revealed Word of God (John 1:1). The other word is "rhema."

There is only one Word of God, but the emphasis of rhema is in its expression. We are to hide the whole Word (logos) in our hearts, and when Satan attacks, we stand against him by confessing God's Word (rhema). Confessing what we believe gives proof to our faith. Confession doesn't create faith; faith makes possible true confession. Confession is agreeing with God. It is living in the light by letting our life and our mouth demonstrate what we believe in our hearts.

E. WE MUST BELIEVE TO RECEIVE

"And what is the exceeding greatness of his power to us-ward who believe, according to the working of his mighty power" (Ephesians 1:19). We need to not only know God's power, but the greatness of God's power, and then the exceeding greatness of God's power. This exceeding greatness of God's power is towards us.

That means that it is for us and for our benefit. Some people get glimpses of God's power, but very few have the revelation that it is for us and at our disposal. It doesn't do us any good to believe that God has power if we don't believe that it will work for us. This great power of God is effectual only for those who believe. We must believe to receive, or if we doubt, we do without.

F. JESUS WON THE VICTORY FOR US

"And whatsoever ye shall ask in my name, that will I do, that the Father may be glorified in the Son. If ye shall ask any thing in my name, I will do it" (John 14:13-14). Once again, we are told to ask and it will be done as we request. Ask anything, Jesus says. But ask it in My name, He cautions us. Why in His name? Because Jesus won the victory for us and holds all power in heaven and on earth. When we ask in the name of Jesus, we are asking as a representative and as a follower of Jesus. Therefore, our asking has to be in line with the way Jesus would ask. What does this mean? It means we must ask believing. And we must believe not only that God can do what we ask but also that God wants to do what we ask.

Jesus was always in agreement with God's will. He never asked God for something that He knew to be outside of God's will. Jesus forgave people's sins and he healed all who received Him. He did not turn some away because God did not want a particular person to be forgiven or a particular person to be healed. Jesus knew that God wanted them all forgiven and God wanted them all healed. God was glorified because His Son faithfully performed the works of the Father. And God is glorified when each of us acts as a vessel for Jesus to continue to do the works of the Father.

Part "B"

❧❧

Chapter 5

A. REST IS NOT OPTIONAL

"And he said unto them, Come ye yourselves apart into a desert place, and rest a while: for there were many coming and going, and they had no leisure so much as to eat" (Mark 6:31). One of Satan's deadliest weapons against those involved in ministry is busyness.

We must balance our time ministering to others with our time being ministered to by our Father. If the devil can't stop you from "getting on fire" for God, then he'll try to stop you by getting you "burned out." Remember, the reason Jesus and His disciples were going to this remote place was to get away from the multitude for a while and rest. This rest was not optional, but rather a necessity.

B. YOU ARE AN AMBASSADOR FOR CHRIST

Heaven is just waiting to act on your behalf. Why? Because you are an ambassador for Christ to this world! In 2 Corinthians 5:20, Paul wrote, "Now then we are ambassadors for Christ…"

We are heavenly delegates—"ambassadors" who have been sent forth as Heaven's representatives to planet earth! As ambassadors for Christ, we are the voice of Heaven. As His representatives, we are authorized to speak and act on behalf of the Lord. And as Heaven's ambassadors, we are fully backed, fully funded, fully defended, and fully assisted by the authority and resources of Heaven!

C. MOST PEOPLE TELL GOD ABOUT THEIR PROBLEMS

Matthew 12:37: "For by thy words thou shalt be justified, and by thy words thou shalt be condemned." If we begin to speak words in faith that line up with God's Word, then positive results will follow. If we continue to speak words of doubt, we will eventually believe them and have the negative things that these words produce. Death or life is in the power of every word we speak. Faith is released by speaking words.

Jesus encouraged us to speak to mountains or to whatever our problem is. Most people speak to God about their problems, but few follow Jesus' instructions and speak directly to the "mountain." God has put certain things under our authority and we must exercise it. When a problem stands in our way, we must speak to the problem and command it to get out of our way in the name of Jesus. Speak God's Word today. His Words will produce life.

D. THE MYSTERIES OF THE KINGDOM OF HEAVEN

Matthew 13:11: "He answered and said unto them, Because it is given unto you to know the mysteries of the kingdom of heaven, but to them it is not given." Jesus is speaking about those who have revelation knowledge of the mysteries of God. They will receive even more revelation and will walk in the abundant life that Jesus provided (Jn. 10:10; 2 Pet. 1:3).

Those who do not receive God's revelation will lose whatever truth they do have and will go further into deception. God reveals His truths to us in stages, not all at once (Isa. 28:9-10). Therefore, as we walk in the revelation of what the Lord has already shown us, He will reveal more of His truths to us. The truths of God are mysterious only to those who do not soften their hearts by seeking God with their whole hearts. As Jeremiah 29:13 says, "And ye shall seek me, and find me, when ye shall search for me with all your heart."

E. TOTAL VICTORY IS YOURS

It's not the Bible lying on your coffee table that makes the enemy flee, but it is the Word of God hidden in your heart, activated by the power of the Holy Spirit, and spoken in an appropriate situation. It's similar to what was spoken by Jesus in John 6:63: "...the words that I speak unto you, they are spirit and they are life." The Word by itself doesn't make us free. It is the Word we know and speak that will deliver us (Jn. 8:32).

Why is the Word so effective? It's because it is the WORD of God. It has authority, because it is indeed the WORD of God. God's Word supersedes all authority of the Church, of reason, of intellect, and even of Satan. It is the Holy Spirit that wields this Word as it is spoken in faith. Speaking God's Word in faith brings the Holy Spirit into action. In Luke, chapter four, when Jesus was tempted of the devil for 40 days, it was the Word of God that Jesus used to defeat the enemy in the time of His temptation. Jesus constantly met His temptation by quoting from God's Word as He repeatedly stated the phrase, "It is written." Likewise, the Christian soldier must avail himself of God's Word by placing it in his heart, so that the Holy Spirit may bring it forth at the appropriate time to accomplish a complete and total victory. It's yours!

F. JESUS WANTS JOY TO REIGN IN YOUR HEART

People who become ill often have an underlying anger, grief, shame, or fear. True healing cannot occur until these wounds are acknowledged and healed. Sometimes these hurts are buried very, very deeply because they are so painful. These wounds didn't come from God. They have accumulated through strife, loss, and hurtful life experiences.

As a result, many of us have a myriad of negative emotions that the destroyer encourages us to hold on to. Don't keep struggling with your emotional scars. God has provided the solution and victory—deliverance through the authority of Luke 10:19. Jesus came to heal the broken-hearted and to set at liberty those that are bruised. He wants you to be completely whole. He wants joy to reign in your heart. He smiles at you with compassion and offers His hand of deliverance, freedom, and peace.

Part "B"

❧

Chapter 6

A. FAITHFULNESS IN THE SMALL THINGS

"He that receiveth you, receiveth me" (Matthew 10:40). Honor or contempt put upon an ambassador reflects honor or contempt upon the prince that sends him, and ministers are ambassadors for Christ. Many people are waiting for the important jobs to come along where they can make a big impact or receive a lot of recognition, while they pass by the lesser opportunities.

In the kingdom of God, we won't be given any great opportunities until we are proven faithful in the small things (Luke 16:10). Today, ask the Lord to show you ways you can minister to others by serving them.

B. HIS RESURRECTION POWER

"Come unto me, all ye that labour and are heavy laden, and I will give you rest" (Matthew 11:28). Notice that Jesus doesn't say He will come to you. He says that you must choose to go to Him! But if you will make the deliberate choice to wait upon the Lord, Jesus promises that you will find this promised rest.

So come into the Presence of God and allow Him to refresh you. As you do, the Holy Spirit will release His resurrection power and you will be quickened in your physical body (Ephesians 1:18-20).

C. PEOPLE ARE LOOKING AT HOW WE LIVE

The way that you can tell whether a person is genuine is by the fruit he produces. This fruit is his lifestyle (Matt. 7:20)

Jesus contrasts the good tree and its good fruit and the bad tree and its evil fruit. He emphasizes the impossibility of an evil tree bearing good fruit—we never mistake a tree seeing its fruit. Look at the fruit. Fruit is the true test of ministers and ministries. If people are being saved, if lives are being changed, there is good fruit.

Even though the minister may say something bad and make mistakes, the fruit is good. Therefore, you can say that the tree is good. When a person says all of the right things and seems sincere, but the lives of the people around him are shattered, torn, and in confusion and distress, then the fruit is bad. You can judge the effectiveness of a person by the fruit he is producing in his life. In ministry you can judge the effectiveness of a minister by the fruit his ministry is producing. Today, make sure that the fruit produced from your life is good fruit. Make sure that you are making a positive impact on people's lives, that you are turning people to the Lord and not leaving them hurt and confused. People are looking at you to see what type of fruit you are bearing.

D. ALWAYS HAVE FAITH, DECLARE GOD'S WORD

Doubtful thoughts will come, but we do not sin until we entertain them. According to this verse, speaking forth these thoughts is one way of entertaining them; therefore, don't speak forth these negative thoughts. It is imperative that we watch the words we say. Begin to speak words in faith that line up with God's Word, and then positive results will follow. If we speak words of doubt, we will eventually believe them and have the negative things that these words produce.

There are no such things as "idle" words that will not work for or against us. Death or life is in the power of every word we speak (Prov. 18:21). Our words can be our most powerful weapon against the devil, or they can become a snare of the devil (Prov. 6:2; Matt. 12:37).

E. THE LOVE OF MONEY IS THE ROOT OF ALL EVIL

"For where your treasure is, there will your heart be also" (Matthew 6:21). If isolated from the rest of God's Word, there are some scriptures that could be interpreted that having money or wealth is wrong; however, there are other scriptures that speak of riches as a blessing. The harmony between these two apparently opposite positions is that money is neither good nor bad.

It is the love of money that is the root of all evil, and many have committed the sin of loving money that don't even have a dime (1 Tim. 6:10). People may have money, and yet not love it, but if they love it excessively, it will push them on to all evil. Covetous persons will quit the faith, if that were the way to get money: Which while some coveted after, they have erred from the faith. "Demas hath forsaken me, having loved this present world" (2 Timothy 4:10).

F. THE BEST PRAYER OF ALl

Remember that Jesus answered, "I will," when the leper asked for healing, "If thou wilt, thou canst make me clean" (Matthew 8:2). God cannot contradict Himself and He always keeps His Word. If He has already done something, already released a perpetual flow of grace and healing toward us, He can't act as though He hasn't done it.

James teaches that it is the prayer of faith that saves, heals, and delivers the sick (James 5:15). A faith-filled prayer is one that is first and foremost in agreement with the Word of God. Be aware of prayers you pray with others. Make sure that you join in agreement with faith-filled, Word-based petitions to the Almighty. The best prayers of all are to speak God's own words back to Him because He is always faithful to perform them.

Part "B"

Chapter 7

A. OPPORTUNITIES ARE ALL AROUND US

Jesus gave us the key to purifying our motives. He said, "But when thou doest alms, let not thy left hand know what thy right hand doeth" (Mt. 6:3). Giving in a manner in which you will not receive recognition for your gifts will guarantee that your motives are right and grant you the true joy that comes through selfless giving (Acts 20:24).

Ask the Lord to show you an opportunity today to give a kind word or a helping hand to someone who will not be able to repay you, and where others will never know about it. This could be a motorist in a traffic jam, a coworker, a spouse, a child who won't even notice your kind deed, or any number of other people. Opportunities are all around us.

B. GET TO KNOW GOD THROUGH HIS WORD

Our five senses were given to us by God and are necessary to help us function in this life, but if we do not renew our minds to acknowledge the limits of the five senses, they will keep us from believing. Faith can perceive things that the senses cannot (Heb. 11:1). The type of faith that Thomas operated in was a human or natural faith that was based on what he could see.

Jesus said there was a greater blessing to be obtained. That greater blessing comes from using a supernatural, God-kind of faith that is based only on God's Word. Jesus and God's Word are one (John 1:1,14). Believing God's Word is not just putting your trust in some printed words on the pages of a book we call the Bible. There is much more involved. It is a relationship with a person, the person behind the words. Get to know Him through His Word.

C. NOTHING IS IMPOSSIBLE WITH GOD

Remember the Hebrew children in the fiery furnace? (Daniel 3:25) How much more impossible can you get than that? Yet God made a way. Look at the resurrection of Lazarus (John 11:43), Jesus walking on the water, and thousands of other examples in Scripture with God doing the "impossible." God is a miraculous God!

Therefore, there's always hope for those who trust in Him. Regardless of where you are now or what situation you find yourself in, God can chart a course for you back into the center of His perfect will. No one is too far gone, and no situation is too desperate for His miraculous intervention!

D. GOD SEES US THROUGH JESUS

When Jesus was raised from the dead, He enabled us to be "born of the Spirit" and become children of God, heirs of God, and joint-heirs with Christ. We were enabled to become "partakers of the divine nature" and full-fledged sons of God. Salvation is not a reformation, but rather regeneration—a new birth, a new creation that can only be accomplished by a creative miracle of the Holy Spirit. Because of the new birth, God sees us through Jesus. Celebrate life.

E. WE WERE SAVED BY FAITH THROUGH IN GOD

"Therefore being justified by faith, we have peace with God through our Lord Jesus Christ" (Romans 5:1). The first benefit of being justified by faith-instead of works that Paul mentioned is peace. Peace comes when we relate to God in faith based on what He did for us instead of what we do for Him.

Those who think we must perform up to some standard to be accepted by God will have no peace. That puts the burden of salvation on our shoulders. We are incapable of living holy enough to please God—before or after salvation (Heb. 11:6). We were saved by faith, and we have to continue to walk with God by faith (Col. 2:6). "As ye have therefore received Christ Jesus the Lord, so walk ye in him." We received it by putting faith in Jesus as our Savior (Eph. 2:8).

Part "B"

⸎

CHAPTER 8

A. BELIEVE THE WORDS OF GOD; THEY ARE POWERFUL
The Word of God Is Life. It is the spirit that quickeneth; the flesh prof-iteth nothing: the words that I speak unto you, they are spirit, and they are life (John 6:63). Jesus tells us that it is the spirit that makes us alive, that vitalizes us. Contrary to that, the body and our human nature profit us nothing. Why would this be? Because God is spirit. Jesus continues: "The words that I speak to you, they are spirit and they are life." Jesus was the Word itself. John 1:1 tells us that "in the beginning was the Word, and the Word was with God, and the Word was God." His words are spirit because God is spirit.

His words are life because God is the life-giver. They are life because Jesus died to defeat Satan and to win perfect victory for us. His words are rhema, which means that through the Living Word, the Lord speaks di-rectly to you. There is life-giving vitality in the Word. The Word of God is Spirit that calls out to your own born-again spirit. Seek out the declared will of God that is revealed in His Holy Word. Let it birth life in you.

B. TREAT YOURSELF TO A HEALTHY SPIRITUAL MEAL

Being carnally minded produces death (Rom. 8:6). Carnal mindedness doesn't just tend towards death. It equals death. And spiritual mindedness doesn't just tend towards life. It equals life. I don't have to be with a person to see what he has been thinking. All I have to do is see the dominant fruit of that person's life and I can tell. It's like looking at a person's garden. What was planted is what grows there.

In our health-conscious society, many of us wouldn't dream of abusing our bodies by having poor diets. Yet in our souls, we are killing ourselves by feeding on the wrong things. Today, treat yourself to a healthy spiritual meal.

C. FAITH DEMANDS ACTION

The Lord gave His Word to the Jews, but they didn't believe it. Hebrews 4:2 says, "... the word preached did not profit them, not being mixed with faith in them that heard [it]." We have been given God's words too, in the Bible. If we will speak God's Word in faith, we will get the same results that Jesus did. God's Word never fails. It is eternal, and not one promise will fall to the ground. But for it to work for us, we have to believe it.

God's Word has all power, but all that power will not be released until we believe it. Many people know God's Word is true and pray for its power to be released in their lives. But it won't happen through desire alone. We have to believe it. Many people are afraid to believe because they know true faith demands actions. It's easier to just pray and then, if nothing happens in the physical, say we are waiting on God. But God is waiting on us to believe.

E. OUR SUCCESS COMES FROM GOD

Our success stems solely from our vital, continual contact with God. That one factor rules all others. If you're in contact with the Lord, those other qualities will flow naturally from you. If you keep a prayerful connection with God, you will walk in love and joy. You will walk in forgiveness. So what exactly is a continual connection with God? It simply means keeping the lines of communication open between the two of you.

It means going about your daily activities in such a way that you're always ready to hear from Him. Just think: The real key to consistent victory is just one thing! You don't have to memorize a list of dos and don'ts. All you have to do is keep in continual contact with God. He's always speaking to our hearts. Keep your ear tuned to Him. Keep your heart lined up with His Word. Just keep the line open! 1 John 1:1-7.

F. THE POWER TO ACT AND SPEAK WITH BOLDNESS

"And when they had prayed, the place was shaken where they were assembled together; and they were all filled with the Holy Ghost, and they spake the word of God with boldness" (Acts 4:31). The Holy Spirit's control and influence over our souls and bodies fluctuates proportionately to how well our minds are renewed to His will (Romans 12:2). Boldness is the outer sign of the possession of the Holy Spirit's anointing.

We need to picture ourselves as bold people. How would we act, what would we say, what would we dare? Perhaps it's an act of love, which we've resisted doing, or an opportunity to share our faith, which has been neglected because of embarrassment or timidity. Or perhaps it's the forgiveness we need to express, or taking a stand and speaking forthrightly what we believe. Most of all, it's following the Lord's guidance with faithfulness and obedience, regardless of cost. Ask for a special infilling of the Holy Spirit. He's faithful. He will give us the power to act and speak with boldness.

PART "B"

CHAPTER 9

A. YOUR MIND CAN BE WORRY-FREE ZONE:

There isn't a shortage of faith. There's just a shortage of people who use the faith God gave them! We can do many things to release the God-given faith that's in us, but before we can do any of them, we must believe the faith is there. Instead of acknowledging your lack today. Set sometimes aside daily to acknowledge the faith of Jesus that you have in your heart; so your mind can be a worry-free zone. This is the first step toward making your faith effective (Philemon. 1:6).

B. YOU SHOULD BE GRACE CONSCIOUS:

Trying to relate to God on the basis of your efforts plus Jesus will hurt you. In fact, the harder you try, the worse it becomes. You just end up living under condemnation in a perpetual cycle of failure and defeat. As a believer, you should be grace conscious. Yet, sadly, many believers today are more conscious of their own sins and the sins of others instead of Jesus, the "Lamb of God who has taken away the sins of the world,"

C. YOU CAN SPEAK DIRECTLY TO THE PROBLEM:

Jesus answered and said unto them, Verily I say unto you, If ye have faith, and doubt not, ye shall not only do this which is done to the fig tree, but also if ye shall say unto this mountain, Be thou removed, and be thou cast into the sea; it shall be done. Matthew 21:21. Notice that Jesus said we should speak to the mountain. Most people are praying to God about their mountain, but the Lord said we should speak directly to it. This reflects our God-given authority. Mountain-moving faith believes that God has already provided healing for us. In Jesus' name, you can speak directly to the problem instead of speaking to God about the problem. Use your God-given authority, and speak to your mountain today. If you believe, it will move.

D. YOU CAN BEGIN TO CHANGE YOUR LIFE:

"Through faith, we understand that the worlds were framed by the word of God, so that things which are seen were not made of things which do appear" (Heb. 11:3). Words are keys that unlock the powers of God's universe. When the words we speak are in line with His Word, His power is released. If we agree with the devil and speak forth his thoughts of doubt, we unleash his power. "Death and life are in the power of the tongue: and they that love it shall eat the fruit thereof" (Prov. 18:21). What words are coming out of your mouth? Are you saying what you have or what you want? If you learn the power of speaking God's Word in faith, you can begin to change your life. Today, pray the prayer David prayed, "Set a watch, O Lord, before my mouth; keep the door of my lips" (Ps. 141:3).

E. YOU ARE SAVED TO SERVE:

If you believe you have to perform to a certain standard or fulfill some duty in order to approach God, you've missed the real message of the cross. You've taken a "form of godliness but denied its power" as Second

Timothy 3:5 says. You're living between two covenants, mixing a little of the New with the Old. Living in the freedom that Christ bought for us and allowing that freedom to produce the right motives (serving from the finished work of Christ). Saved to serve, not saved to be served. Read Ephesian 2:8-10).

PART "B"

CHAPTER 10

A. YOU ARE NOT AN ACCIDENT:

If there was no God, we would all be "accidents," the result of astronomical random chance in the universe. But there is a God who made you for a reason, and your life has profound meaning! We discover that meaning and purpose only when we make Jesus the Lord of our lives, and God the reference point of our lives. The Message paraphrase of Romans 12:3 says, "The only accurate way to understand ourselves is by what God is and by what he does for us." (Read 1 Corinthians 1:9).

B. WHO ARE YOUR FRIENDS?:

Peter denied knowing Jesus when he feared what others might say. And Pilate, even though he knew Jesus had done nothing worthy of punishment, allowed Jesus to be crucified because he feared the disapproval of the crowd. Let me be frank: If your friends are causing you to downplay your commitment to Jesus, deny your beliefs, compromise your values, or give up on the dream God gave you, you need to find new friends! The Bible warns, "Do not follow the crowd in doing wrong." Exodus 23:2 (NIV) It also says, "If bad companions tempt you, don't go along with them." Proverbs 1:10 (MSG) Friends who discourage your walk with God are not true friends. "Do not be misled: 'Bad company corrupts good character.' Come back to your senses as you ought, and stop sinning." 1 Corinthians 1:33-34 (NIV).

C. WHEN FAITH STRENGTHENS, DOUBT WEAKENS:

A poor self-image undermines anyone's possibilities. The devil knows this. He works ceaselessly at imprinting a poor self-image on the minds of people everywhere. If the devil can get us to doubt who we are in Christ, we will be rendered powerless. Doubt needs no help to grow, but faith needs reinforcement every day. As we act in faith every day, we reinforce it constantly. When faith strengthens, doubt weakens.

D. WE HAVE THE MIND OF CHRIST:

It is necessary for us to know what God through the Word and through the Holy Spirit has wrought in us, through the renewing of our mind. We renew our minds by studying the Word of God. The Bible teaches us to have "the mind of Christ" (1 Cor. 2:16). The only way we can have the mind of Christ is to study His Word, believe it in our heart, and act upon it. Our confession is the result of our believing, and our believing is the result of our right or wrong thinking, (read Matt. 7: 24-27).

E. VICTORY OVER FEAR:

How can you tell if your discouragement is being caused by fear? You have a deep, intense desire to run. You have an intense desire to escape from life's demands and pressures. The natural reaction of fear is always to run. In life there are only three ways you can move—against something in anger, away from it in fear, or with it in love. "For God hath not given us the spirit of fear; but of power, and of love, and of a sound mind". 2 Timothy 1:7.

PART "B"

CHAPTER 11

A. USE YOUR DELEGATED AUTHORITY:

Mark 16:17 "And these signs shall follow them that believe; In my name shall they cast out devils; they shall speak with new tongues". We have come to share in His throne (Ephesian 2:6), which means we partake of the authority that His throne represents and exercise divine power and dominion on this earth.

There is no place in the New Testament that tells you to ask God to do something about the devil. Instead, you are told to do something about the devil. This is because you have been delegated His authority over the works of the enemy. Let the eyes of your understanding be enlightened to His exceeding power toward you. (Ephesian 1:18,19.) Today, take authority over the devil, and walk-in victory!

B. THE WONDERFUL NAME OF JESUS:

Three things are necessary in order to pray and take deliverance and victory over demons. First, we must be children of God; because nature determines by birth. Second, we must know the power of the Name of Jesus; because name determines identity. Third, we must not have any unconfessed or unforgiven sin in the heart, for if we do, the demons will laugh at our prayers.

C. THE TRUE NATURE OF GOD:

Loving others is dependent on us knowing God. Our poor relationships with others are indicative of our poor relationship with the Lord. There are many characteristics of God, but God is love. That is the true nature of God. Love isn't just a feeling; it's an action. Love has to be expressed. God expressed His love toward us by giving His only begotten Son as total payment for our sins so we could partake of His life. (1 John 4:8-9).

D. THE STRUGGLE IS OVER:

"As He is now, so am I in this world." It does not require any faith on my part to enjoy my possession (healing, deliverance, and joy), because He gave them to me through His death; it is mine, and what is mine I do not have to have faith to obtain, for I have already obtained them; I am in possession of them. All I need to do is praise Him, and when I praise Him and thank Him, then the things becomes operative in my life. (Read 1 John 4:17; John 10:10; Isaiah 53:4,5).

E. THE SOURCE AND THE SEASON OF REJOICING:

Rejoice in the Lord always: and again I say, Rejoice (Philippians 4:4). Seventeen times the words "rejoice," "rejoiced," "rejoicing" or "joy" are found in the epistle. The source of rejoicing. "In the Lord". This qualified the rejoicing. It is not rejoicing in one's circumstances, which are frequently a cause of anything but joy. It is not rejoicing in a sport's victory or a politician's election victory. It is rejoicing "in the Lord." He is the source of true joy. We would say always with an "s" today. The word means to always be rejoicing "in the Lord." We cannot rejoice in other things always but we can rejoice in the Lord always. There is never a time when you cannot rejoice in the Lord.

PART "B"

⇒⊱

CHAPTER 12

A. THE RIGHT HAND OF GOD:

Fear thou not; for I am with thee: be not dismayed; for I am thy God: I will strengthen thee; yea, I will help thee; yea, I will uphold thee with the right hand of my righteousness, Isaiah 41:10. If we were just on our own, there would be good reason to fear. Life is a terminal experience. Traps and snares are everywhere. But the person who has God with them has good reason not to fear. He has promised to strengthen us, help us, and uphold us with the right hand of His righteousness. The "right hand" is signifying strength and skill. The Lord will use all His strength and skill to uphold us. Notice that not only are we not to fear, but also we are not to be dismayed. The English word "dismay" means "To fill with dread or apprehension; daunt" (American Heritage Dictionary). Dismay would be the beginning stages of fear. It's less than full-blown fear or terror. It's just a dread or apprehension of something bad happening, (read Josh. 1:9).

43

B. THE PRINCIPLE OF RELATIONSHIP:

Therefore, whatever you want men to do to you, do also to them, for this is the Law and the Prophets. Matthew 7:12: The equity in this principle is that you are to treat others as you want them to treat you (it is not treat others as they treat you). This puts everyone on equal terms in our conduct one to another. There is nothing unfair or unjust about this principle. This equity will not allow for hypocrisy-you will not be as some who are resolute about their own rights but have no regard for the rights of others. "Whatsoever." The principle includes every act and every person. It applies to all - the king as well as to the subjects.

C. THE PRINCE OF PEACE:

You will never enjoy complete peace of mind until you have a relationship with the Prince of Peace. Matt. 11:28–30). Christ did not say, "Come to me and I will give you more guilt, more burdens, more stress, and more worries"—even though that's what a lot of people seem to teach! Some churches tend to create pressure rather than relieve it. But Jesus said, "I want to give you rest. I am the Stress-Reliever. When you get in harmony with me, I will give you inner strength." Christ can transform your lifestyle from stressful to satisfied. The greatest source of stress comes from trying to live our lives apart from the God who made us, trying to go our own way and be our own god.

D. THE POWER OF THE WORD OF GOD:

1 Thess. 5:5 Ye are all the children of light, and the children of the day: we are not of the night, nor of darkness. The Word says that believers are the children of light, not of darkness, because we have been born again into God's Kingdom of light. That's why it's so important to walk in the light! Walking in the light of God's Word ensures pro-

tection against all of Satan's evil hosts. The devil can rule over us if we unknowingly through ignorance of God's Word or willingly give him permission to rule over us. That's one reason the Bible exhorts believers to walk in the light! Rulers of darkness can't rule in the light, so they can't rule those who walk in the light! (Read John 8:12,35).

E. THE NAME THAT IS ABOVE OTHERS:

Peter said, Silver and gold have I none; but such as I have to give I thee: In the name of Jesus Christ of Nazareth rise up and walk. Acts 3:6: A name, of course, implies much more than identification; it carries with it authority, reputation, and power. The name of the Lord Jesus has all authority behind it, for He is the Son of God (Matt. 28:18). Because His name is "above every name" (Phil. 2:9-11), He deserves our worship and obedience. The great concern of the first Christians was that the name of Jesus Christ, God's Son, be glorified; and believers today should have that same focus.

F. THE KEY TO PEACE OF MIND:

Looking unto Jesus the author and finisher of our faith; ...Hebrews 12:2. Instead of focusing on that unappeasable person, refocus on Jesus, who accepts you unconditionally. The more important Jesus becomes to you, the freer you will be from the disapproval of others. Jesus promised it. He said, "If the Son sets you free, you will be free indeed." John 8:36. Getting to know Jesus personally and intimately can freer you from many things: the burden of guilt, the poison of resentment, the stress of overwork, the pressure of materialism, the habits of addiction, and the fear of death. But one of the greatest freedoms Jesus offers is being liberated from the fear of disapproval. That is a key to peace of mind.

CHAPTER 13

A. THE GOSPEL IS THE POWER OF GOD:

For I am not ashamed of the gospel of Christ: for it is the power of God unto salvation to everyone that believeth; to the Jew first, and also to the Greek. Romans 1:16, The Gospel is the power of God that releases the effects of salvation in our lives. Salvation is much more than just being born again. This refers to every benefit that the believer is entitled to through Jesus. Therefore, if we are not experiencing the abundance that Jesus provided for us in any area of our lives-then we are having a problem understanding and/or believing the Gospel.

B. THE CALL TO PRAYER:

The call to prayer is the Father's invitation to visit with Him. It is the call of Love to come and Fellowship. Prayer is the voice of Faith to the Father. Prayer is born then of the sense of need, and the assurance that the need will be met. Unbelief cannot pray; it can only utter words.

Prayer is the Living Word in lips of faith. When we quote the Word, we quote Him. When we rest on the Word, we rest on the finished work of Christ. His Word is my contact with Him. (Read 1 John 5:14).

C. SUPERNATURAL INTERVENTION:

For much of the Church, Calvary is mainly about God forgiving our sins. People stop short of understanding and walking in the full purpose for Jesus' death, which was to restore us to relationship with Him and to the identity that He intended for us from the beginning.

To progress in your understanding of God's deep purposes for you, seek ongoing encounters with your Father so that you can hear Him declare over you how He values you. Our boldness to declare and demonstrate who He is in a given situation is seriously impaired if we're not confident of who we are in Him. When the boldness that is normal to the one filled with the Spirit of God diminishes, it costs us dearly. It is often our boldness that draws Him into an impossible situation (read 1 John 4:17).

D. SET ASIDE, SOMETIMES TO SPEND WITH THE LORD:

Come unto me, all ye that labor and are heavily laden, and I will give you rest. — Matthew 11:28. I am convinced that one reason, why the devil has access to people's emotions is that they keep flying through life without taking time to get renewed in the Presence of the Lord. They ignore their need to sit, to rest, and to wait upon the Lord. As a result, their perception of things around them gets blurred.

E. SEEK OUT THE DECLARED WILL OF GOD THAT IS REVEALED IN HIS WORD:

The Word of God Is Life It is the spirit that quickeneth; the flesh profiteth nothing: the words that I speak unto you, they are spirit, and they are life, (John 6: 63). Jesus tells us that it is the spirit that makes us alive, that vitalizes us. Contrary to that, the body and our human nature profit us nothing. Why would this be? Because God is spirit. Jesus continues. "The words that I speak to you, they are spirit and they are life." Jesus was the Word itself. John 1: 1 tells us that "in the beginning was the Word, and the Word was with God, and the Word was God." His words are spirit because God is spirit.

His words are life because God is the life-giver. They are life because Jesus died to defeat Satan and to win perfect victory for us. His words are rhema, which means that through the Living Word, the Lord speaks directly to you. There is life-giving vitality in the Word. The Word of God is Spirit that calls out to your own born-again spirit. Seek out the declared will of God that is revealed in His Holy Word. Let it birth life in you.

F. YOU ARE A NEW CREATION:

Satan is not only conquered, but God has made you a New Creation over whom Satan has no dominion whatsoever. 2 Corinthians 5:17-18, "Wherefore if any man is in Christ, he is a new creation: the old things are passed away; behold, they become new. But all these things (victory, power, authority) are of God, who reconciled us to himself through Christ, and gave unto us the ministry of reconciliation." Those old things are the things of defeat, failure, weakness, poverty, sin, and spiritual death. We are New Creations. Jesus is the head of this New Creation. Be cheerful we are on the winner's side.

PART "B"

✴

CHAPTER 14

A. THE IMPORTANCE OF FAITH:

The importance of faith in the finished work of Christ: No matter what a man's privileges are if the hand of faith is paralyzed he cannot take hold of them. As long as he is ruled by sin-consciousness, he has no sense of Redemption. He is under condemnation. Satan rules him. As long as Satan rules, faith will be shriveled and undeveloped. The soul contacts the intellectual realm, the physical body contacts the physical realm, and the spirit, the spiritual realm. Luke 21:19 (KJV) In your patience possess ye your souls.

B. TEACHINGS ON PRAYER, FASTING AND OTHERS:

Biblical themes such as prayer, fasting, gifts of the Spirit, prosperity, healing, marriage, ethics, etc., must be presented within the essential framework of the revelation of redemption (the finished work of Christ). It is the principle of Scripture by which all biblical doctrine is measured. It is vital that we comprehend the redemptive reasons why God's provisions and His power are available to us as believers in Christ, (read Colossians 1:12-14). Will you answer His call into the great harvest?

C. PRAYER WORKS:

"And this is the confidence that we have in him, that, if we ask any thing according to his will, he heareth us", 1 John 5:14. Prayer means that we have come boldly into the throne room and are standing in His presence. It is more than bringing Him on the scene. It is going into the presence of the Father and Jesus in an executive meeting, laying our needs before them and making our requisitions for ability, for grace, healing for someone, or victory for someone, or for financial needs. Whatever that need may be, we are making a demand upon Him. (Read Hebrews 4:16).

D. "MEN OUTHT ALWAYS TO PRAY AND NOT FAINT":

Prayer is facing God with man's needs, with His promise to meet those needs. He taught us to pray. He taught us to trust His Word. Prayer is a part of God's program for us. He encourages us to act on His Word. He is one with us in this prayer life. It is His way of saving, healing, and blessing men. Jesus said in Luke 18:1: "Men ought always to pray and not faint."

E. OUR WORDS CAN BE OUR MOST POWERFUL WEAPON:

Therefore, take no thought, saying, What shall we eat? or, What shall we drink? or, Wherewithal shall we be clothed? Matthew 6:31. According to this verse, the way we take an anxious thought is by speaking it. Doubtful thoughts will come, but we do not sin until we entertain them and declare them. Speaking these thoughts is one way of entertaining them; therefore, don't speak any anxious thoughts! There are no such things as "idle" words that will not work for or against us. Death or life is in the power of every word we speak. (Prov. 18:21.) Our words can be our most powerful weapon to release the power of God and defeat the devil, or they can become a snare of the devil. (Prov. 6:2.).

F. OUR CONTINUAL CONTACT WITH GOD:

Our success stems solely from our vital, continual contact with God. That one factor rules all others. If you're in contact with the Lord, those other qualities will flow naturally from you. If you keep a prayerful connection with God, you will walk in love and joy. You will walk in forgiveness. So what exactly is a continual connection with God? It simply means keeping the lines of communication open between the two of you.

It means going about your daily activities in such a way that you're always ready to hear from Him. Just think: The real key to consistent victory is just one thing! You don't have to memorize a list of dos and don'ts. All you have to do is keep in continual contact with God. He's always speaking to our hearts. Keep your ear tuned to Him. Keep your heart lined up with His Word. Just keep the line open! 1 John 1:1-7.

PART "B"

CHAPTER 15

A. OUR FIRST PRIORITY AS BELIEVERS:

When our eyes are steadfastly fixed on God, He brings everything else into our sphere. Jesus stated it this way: But seek ye first the kingdom of God, and his righteousness; and all these things shall be added unto you. Matthew 6:33. Our first priority as believers is to seek the Kingdom and righteousness of God. If we do that, He will see to it that we receive all those other things. The key is to fix our attention on God's will, God's Word, and God's glory, and trust Him for the rest. This knowledge comes through God's Word and from spending time in His presence.

B. ONE OF THE ENEMIES OF PRAYER IS DOUBT:

When we doubt God's Word, it is because we believe something else that is contrary to that Word. Our confidence may be in the arm of flesh; it may be in institutions; but whatever our confidence is in, if it contradicts the Word it destroys our faith life. It destroys our prayers.

Until you know what actually belongs to you in Christ. You will never have a prayer life beyond the baby experience.

C. KNOWING GODLY AND UNGODLY COUNSEL:

Not all ungodly counsel comes from the ungodly. While they mean well, some people lack the faith perspective that you strive for and tend to work to make you more like them than they do to actually try to help you to become stronger in your trust in God.

Your job is to protect yourself from such an influence, especially when you are vulnerable. Your heart is a garden. Some people are good at planting weeds, while others plant the Kingdom. My job, and yours, is to know the difference (read Proverbs 22:24-25).

D. LIVING A HEALTHY CHRISTIAN LIFE:

Finding identity in Christ and the knowledge of your true worth brings freedom from judgment, condemnation, and insecurity. That paradigm shift will allow you to act each day within the scope of who you are truly meant to be with full knowledge of your true value. The price Jesus paid for you on the cross is the highest price possible, so you are worth so much more than any worldly accomplishment can express. Understanding the value you have in Christ is vital to living a healthy Christian life (read Romans 8:1, 37; Ephesians 1:16-18).

E. LITTLE IS MUCH WHEN GOD IS IN IT:

So Jesus said to them, "Because of your unbelief; for assuredly, I say to you, if you have faith as a mustard seed, you will say to this mountain, 'Move from here to there,' and it will move, and nothing will be impossible for you - Matthew 17:20. All we need to move our mountains every day is faith as small as a mustard seed. The mustard seed is one of the tiniest seeds found in Israel. Jesus used the mustard seed parable to make the point that little is much when God is in it. The conclusion is that when we take small steps of faith, we can accomplish great things.

F. BENEFIT OF LISTENING TO GOD:

Listening is what enables us to establish agreement with Him through obeying His voice, and our agreement is what releases heavenly strength and resources into our lives and circumstances. The standard we set for our ears also determines our ability to strengthen ourselves because strengthening ourselves begins with our choice to listen to God's voice more than any other. Therefore, by purposefully associating with people who share our values and controlling our interactions with people who don't, we strengthen ourselves. We need to be careful about who is close to us and gives input into our lives (read Mark 4:24).

PART "B"

CHAPTER 16

A. JESUS MINISTERED IN MERCY:

"The Spirit of the LORD is upon Me, Because He has anointed Me To preach the gospel to the poor; He has sent Me to heal the broken-hearted, To proclaim liberty to the captives And recovery of sight to the blind, To set at liberty those who are oppressed; Luke 4:18. One of the ways that God's goodness is revealed is in mercy. We may describe mercy as the readiness of God to relieve the misery of fallen creatures. The Jews were used to the judgment of the law, but Jesus came to minister grace and truth (Jn. 1:17). the Bible says, But God, who is rich in mercy, for his great love wherewith he loved us, Ephesians 2:4. Thank God for His mercy, and go out and show it to orders.

B. JESUS DESTROYED PRICIPALITIES & POWERS:

And having spoiled principalities and powers, he made a shew of them openly, triumphing over them in it, Colossians 2:15: Jesus not only conquered Satan and his forces but He spoiled them. He stripped them of all their power and authority. He also made an exhibit of them. This was what God did with the devil. He totally spoiled him, and Satan is void of any power or authority to oppress us anymore. But the problem is that much of the body of Christ have missed the parade. They don't know Satan has been defeated. Sadly, many churches are the agent of Satan"s intimidation through their wrong teachings on his authority. We must show them this parade through the pages of the Scripture so they will not live in fear of a defeated foe. That is the purpose of palm Sunday.

C. JESUS CAME TO DELIVER US FROM SIN:

Jesus came to free us from the control of sin, but also the guilt that accompanied it. Our everyday lives should not be consumed with thinking about sin. Neither should regret for all the stupid things we've done fill our days and nights. Jesus gave us freedom—not just freedom from sin but freedom from guilt, shame, and condemnation. We no longer need to be concerned with judgment. We do not need to be afraid that God will discover our sin. Sin is not on God's mind! (Read Hebrews 9:14; Mark 1:21).

D. INTIMACY WITH THE LORD:

"I am the vine, ye are the branches: He that abideth in me, and I in him, the same bringeth forth much fruit: for without me ye can do nothing", John 15:5: Abiding in the Lord certainly demands intimacy that cannot be achieved without time spent alone with the Lord. But we must also learn to be in communion with the Lord during our daily activities. It is unrealistic and not God's will for us to try to live lives of total seclusion. But we can bring every thought under the control and into subjection to the mind of Christ (2 Corinthians 10:3-5).

E. IN THE NAME OF JESUS:

"Giving thanks always for all things in the Name of our Lord Jesus Christ to God, even the Father." Eph. 5:20. Even our praises and our worship cannot go to God direct: they must come in the Name of our Lord Jesus Christ. We have the right to use that Name against our enemies. We have the right to use it in our petitions. We have the right to use it in our praises and worship. That Name has been given unto us. (Read John 16:23; Mark 16:17).

F. I WILL THANK THE LORD AT ALL TIMES:

Worship is not a part of your life; it is your life. Worship is not just for church services. We are told to "worship him continually" and to "praise him from sunrise to sunset." In the Bible people praised God at work, at home, in battle, in jail, and even in bed! Praise should be the first activity when you open your eyes in the morning and the last activity when you close them at night. David said, "I will thank the Lord at all times. My mouth will always praise him." (1 Cor.10:31 (NIV); Psa. 119:147; 5:3).

Part "B"

❧❧

Chapter 17

A. HOW TO MAKE THE RIGHT DECISION:

Know what you're trying to accomplish. Unless you plan your life and set priorities, you will be pressured by other people to do what they think is important. Every day, either you live by priorities or you live by pressures. There is no other option. Either you decide what is important in your life, or you let other people decide what is important in your life. Busyness is not necessarily productivity. You may be spinning in circles, but you're not accomplishing anything. Preparation causes you to be at ease. To put it another way, preparation prevents pressure but procrastination produces it.

B. HOW TO BREAK FREE:

How to Break Free from the People-Pleaser: If what I do pleases God, I can stop worrying about everyone else's reactions. Even if you could make everyone like you, it wouldn't be a good idea. It would only mean that you have no convictions you deeply believe in and no principles

63

you are willing to stand for. Jesus said, "Woe to you when all men speak well of you!". Luke 6:26. Remember that I don't need anyone's approval to rejoice; Joy is the fruit of the spirit; therefore, joy is a choice; you have it in your spirit, what other people think of you cannot rob your joy unless you allow them to rob it, read Philippians 4:4).

C. HOW TO BECOME MIGHTY IN PRAYER:

"Let us hold fast the confession of our hope without wavering, for He who promised is faithful". Hebrews 10:23 (NKJV) Our faith is measured by our confessions. There is the confession of our heart, and the confession of our lips. When the confession of our lips perfectly harmonizes with the confession of our hearts, and these two confessions confirm God's Word, then we become mighty in our prayer life.

D. HOW TO BE STRONG IN THE LORD:

Lack of understanding of Righteousness, what it is, and what it gives, holds more people in bondage than perhaps anything else. Man cannot deal with the sin problem. He cannot make himself Righteous. These can only come through the finished work of Christ. When we become conscious that we are Righteous in Christ, we will not think of our weaknesses and failings, (read Isaiah 32:17; Ephesians 6:10).

E. HOW TO BE STRONG IN FAITH:

For what does the Scripture say? "Abraham believed God, and it was accounted to him for righteousness." Romans 4:3 (NKJV): Faith is a direct result of what you think on. If you think of God's Word, faith comes. If you think of other things, unbelief and fear come. If you want the faith of Abraham working in you, then think the way he thought and never consider anything except God's Word, and you will be strong in faith. Read Romans 4:19, and meditate on the Promises of God daily with prayer.

F. HEALTHY CONSCIENCE TOWARDS OTHERS:

Jesus came to free us from the control of sin, but also the guilt that accompanied it. Our everyday lives should not be consumed with thinking about sin. Neither should regret all the stupid things we've done to fill our days and nights. What we must do is learn to discern the difference between a healthy conscience towards others and the destructive emotions of condemnation and guilt towards God. (Isaiah 53: 4-5; Hebrews 9:14).

PART "B"

CHAPTER 18

A. GOD'S LOVE DOESN'T KEEP SCORE:

Thinks no evil, 1 Corinthians 13:5. Thinking about evil only gives fuel to the fires of self-pity, anger, and bitterness that Satan wants to ignite within us. Thinking about the wrongs we suffer from others magnifies the offense until it becomes bigger than it actually is. to take a small, splinter-size offense, magnify it to the size of a baseball bat, and then beat our brains out with it. Don't let him do it to you. Decide today to quit keeping score of all the offenses that come your way. Forgive and go on, thinking instead on things that are pure, lovely, and of good report. (Phil. 4:8.) Then you'll enjoy His peace. (Isa. 26:3).

B. GOD DIDN'T TURN HIS BACK ON YOU:

This means that anyone who belongs to Christ has become a new person. The old life is gone; a new life has begun! 2 Corinthians 5:17 (NLT). The moment you understand (by revelation) what Christ has done, everything changes. Your opinion of God changes, your opinion

67

of yourself and others changes as well. You realize God didn't turn His back on you; He always loved you and thought so much of you that He gave up His own Son to have an intimate relationship with you.

C. GOD WILL NEVER REJECT YOU:

When the opinions of others loom large in your life, God's role in your life is reduced. But when God's approval matters most to you, the views of others lose their grip on your life. Whose opinion matters most to you? Whoever that person is, is your god. When you value anyone's opinions more than God's, you give that person power and authority that belongs only to God. That creates all kinds of insecurity within you. On the other hand, when God's approval matters the most to you, it sets you free from insecurity, because he will never reject you, (read Acts 5:29).

D. FROM FAITH TO FAITH:

Many people never even take the first step to faith in Christ because they fear their friends or family will disapprove or look down on them. That is a fatal mistake. The Bible says, "You try to get praise from each other, but you do not try to get the praise that comes from the only God. So how can you believe?" John 5:44 (NCV). Never allow anyone else to stand in the way of your relationship with Christ. People-pleasing is an emotional handicap. It immobilizes your potential. The Message paraphrase of Proverbs 29:25 says, "The fear of human opinion disables." Of course, any fear will hinder you from what God intended for you.

E. FOCUS MORE ON YOUR NEW IDENTITY IN CHRIST:

Low-self-esteem is a common disempowering belief. Many of us spend more time defending and renewing our minds with the belief that we are "not enough," rather than creating a belief based on our new identity in Christ the truth that God never asks us to do something that is not in our new nature to accomplish; because we cannot consistently do what we don't believe we are, we would be wise to focus more on our new identity than on our actions. Philippians 4:13 (AMP) I have strength for all things in Christ Who empowers me [I am ready for anything and equal to anything through Him Who infuses inner strength into me; I am self-sufficient in Christ's sufficiency].

F. FASTING CASTS OUT UNBELIEF:

Mark 9: 29, Jesus said unto them, this kind can come forth by nothing, but by prayer and fasting. Fasting was always used as a means of seeking God to the exclusion of all else. It does not cast out demons, but rather it casts out unbelief. Fasting is beneficial in every aspect of the Christian life—not only in casting out unbelief. The real virtue of a fast is in humbling yourself through self-denial (Ps. 35:13; 69:10), and that can be accomplished through ways other than total abstinence. Partial fasts can be beneficial, as well as, fasts of your time or pleasures. However, because appetite for food is one of your strongest drives, fasting from food seems to get the job done the quickest.

PART "B"

CHAPTER 19

A. FAITH IS A BYPRODUCT OF GOD'S LOVE:

For in Jesus Christ neither circumcision availeth anything, nor uncircumcision; but faith which worketh by love, Galatians 5:6. When we have a clear revelation of God's love for us, faith comes naturally. Faith is a byproduct of God's love. Those who don't believe that God will act on their behalf are people who don't understand His love for them. Faith works when we know the great love God has for us. (Read 1 John 4:8).

B. FAITH DEMANDS ACTIONS:

The Lord gave His Word to the Jews, but they didn't believe it. Hebrews 4:2 says, "... the word preached did not profit them, not being mixed with faith in them that heard [it]." We have been given God's words too, in the Bible. If we will speak God's Word in faith, we will get the same results that Jesus did. God's Word never fails. It is eternal, and not one promise will fall to the ground. But for it to work for us, we have to believe it.

God's Word has all power, but all that power will not be released until we believe it. Many people know God's Word is true and pray for its power to be released in their lives. But it won't happen through desire alone. We have to believe it. Many people are afraid to believe because they know true faith demands actions. It's easier to just pray and then if nothing happens in the physical, say we are waiting on God. But God is waiting on us to believe.

C. DON'T GIVE PLACE TO THE DEVIL:

Thinking thoughts of guilt and condemnation allow Satan to take advantage of believers and keep them in bondage to his lies. Bondage to wrong thoughts hinders believers from standing in their place of authority in Christ and exercising their rightful authority over the devil. In reality, believers are triumphant over the devil and his weapons of accusation because Jesus triumphed over Satan in the Cross (Col. 2:15). But if believers don't stand in that authority, the devil will dominate them. But the Bible says, "Neither give place to the devil" (Eph. 4:27). We are not to let the devil into our thinking.

D. DON'T AVOID RESPONSIBILITY:

If He is as good as many claims, how we respond to this truth will require massive change in how we do life. Instead of creating doctrines that explain away our weakness and anemic faith, we'll actually have to find out why the "greater works than these" have not been happening in and around us (see John 14:12).

Creating doctrines of no miracles today not only contradicts His Word, it is a sneaky way to avoid responsibility. Instead of changing the standard for life given by Jesus, who walked the earth two thousand years ago, we are to embrace it and follow His model.

PART "B"

⇒⇐

CHAPTER 20

A. AGGRESSIVE TYPE OF FAITH:

When she had heard of Jesus, came in the press behind, and touched his garment, Mark 5:27. Notice that Jesus didn't touch this woman; she touched Jesus. Those with an aggressive type of faith make a demand on the Lord instead of just waiting for Him to do something for them. This is similar to the disciples in Matthew 14 when He came to them walking on the water but made as though He would have passed them (Mark 6:48). If they hadn't cried out to Him, He would have walked right on by. Many people don't receive their miracles because they are too passive. The multitude was thronging Him. There is no way this woman could have just stooped over and touched the hem of His garment in a crowd like this. This implies she was on her hands and knees, pressing through the crowd. She was determined. That's why she got healed.

B. DO NOT SET GOALS INDEPENDENT OF GOD:

The Bible advocates vision and goal setting, but we need to exercise wisdom. We shouldn't set goals arbitrarily, independent of God. Establishing goals contrary to His will just absorbs all our time and keeps us from Him. We need to seek God with prayer and fasting just like Anna did, (read Luke 2:37; John 15:5) and find out who we are in Christ and what is our purpose in life. "In Christ" is the place for security. "Christ in us" is the ground for joy and peace.

C. CONSTANT COMMUNION WITH GOD:

It is a constant communion with the Father and it enriches one spiritually. It illumines the Word and illumines the mind, and it freshens and heals the body. A strange feature about this prayer life is that it reaches the uttermost parts of the earth. Now in Heb. 4:16, he tells us to come boldly to the Throne of Grace; that means to come boldly into the Holy of Holies; to come with freedom into the very Presence of God. Now our hearts can understand Mark 15:38: "And the veil of the temple was rent in two from the top to the bottom." In other words, God the Father is no longer shut in alone. He can be approached. He can be met.

D. CONFESSING IS THE PROOF OF OUR FAITH:

To maintain our victory over satan, we must speak forth the Word of God, which is the sword of the Spirit (Ephesians 6:17). In our English translations, two different words are used for the "Word" of God. The most common is logos and it indicates the whole revealed Word of God (John 1:1). The other word is rhema. There is only one Word of God, but the emphasis of rhema is in its expression.

We are to hide the whole Word (logos) in our hearts, and when Satan attacks, we stand against him by confessing God's Word (rhema). Confessing what we believe gives proof to our faith. Confession doesn't create faith; faith makes possible true confession. Confession is agreeing with God. It is living in the light by letting our life and our mouth demonstrate what we believe in our hearts.

E. THE AUTHOR OF OUR SALVATION IS JESUS:

Christ Jesus is the "author of eternal salvation" (Hebrews 5:9) and the "author and finisher of our faith" (Hebrews 12:2). What does it mean to be the "author of eternal salvation"? Jesus initiated, generated, produced, upholds, and sustains the salvation of all mankind. He is the sole Source of our redemption. He's the Finisher of your faith. He didn't just start your faith; He'll see it to the end until it is complete. He will cause you to grow up to the full measure of His purpose for you so that you look just like Him. (See 2 Corinthians 3:18; Ephesians 4:13.). Fellowship with Him, so He can manifest His glory through Him (1 Cor. 1:9).

F. DON'T LET YOUR BUSYNESS LEADS TO A BREAKDOWN:

There's a big problem with moving so fast. The demands of our schedule start piling up, each overlaying the other as we race from place to place. Eventually, our busyness leads to a breakdown of everything. Let's face it — it's extremely difficult to do everything simultaneously. You may be able to swing it for a while, but in time, you'll start missing important details, even getting emotional over unemotional issues because you've pushed yourself beyond your limit. If this is you, slow down and set aside some time to spend with the Lord (Isaiah 40:31).

Part "B"

Chapter 21

A. CONSTANTLY CHANGING YOUR ATTITUDES

Now your attitudes and thoughts must all be constantly changing for the better. Ephesians 4:23 (TLB): it is not good enough to just learn facts from God's Word and store those facts so that we can recall them. We have to meditate on the truths of God's Word until our outlook, feelings, sentiments, and dispositions have been renewed to God's way of thinking. Read Ephesians 4:24: Notice the use of the word "created." As believers, our righteousness and holiness are not something that we grow into. We were created that way when we were born again (John 3:3). This righteousness and holiness are in the new spirits that we received from God. We must continue working out this righteousness and holiness in our actions daily.

B. BEING ESTABLISHED IN THE LOVE OF GOD:

The basis of our relationship with God is to be loved not our love for Him but His love for us. In (I Jn 4: 19) " We love Him, because he first loved us." No matter how you look at this, the love of God is the foundation for everything in the Bible, and the love of God is the beginning and end of everything concerning our Christian lives. Being established in the love of God or walking in the love of God is about walking and living in the love that God has toward us first, and then and only then can we ever dream about loving others.

C. BECOME CO-LABORERS WITH THE LORD:

If our minds are not renewed to cooperate with His purposes, we will still be using the "stinking thinking" of our carnal man, which, as Paul tells us, is "enmity against God" (Rom. 8:7). It is a sobering thing, but we either have our minds renewed, and become co-laborers with the Lord, or our minds are set against Him! There is no neutral ground. Rejecting the mind of Christ quenches the Holy Spirit and sabotages the building He is doing in our lives.

D. APPROPRIATE THE LOVE OF GOD IN CHRIST:

Are you short-tempered with others? Do you constantly find fault with everything? It's possible that the problem really isn't with others, but with you. Are you upset with yourself? Are you never satisfied with your own performance? Have you not found true forgiveness in the grace of God? We can't control what others around us do, but we can control ourselves. As we appropriate the love of God that's available to us personally, we'll be able to extend that love to others. If we are void of God's love, it'll show in our treatment of others (read 1 Cor. 13:8; 1John4:20).

E. GOD WANTS YOU TO PROSPER & HEALTHY:

Beloved, I wish above all things that YOU may prosper and be in health, even as thy soul prosper, 3 John 1:2: Notice that this prosperity happens as our souls prosper. We can't really prosper outwardly if we aren't prospering inwardly. Our spirits are already perfect (2 Corinthians 5:17), but our souls (the seat of our emotions, wills, and minds) only prosper as we renew our minds (part of the soul) to what we already have in Christ (in our born-again spirits) (read Romans 12:2). I believe that the greatest determinant of mental and spiritual health and spiritual freedom is a true understanding of God and a right relationship with Him. Good theology is an indispensable prerequisite to good psychology. The New Birth is instantaneous, but the renewing of our mind is a gradual process. Its growth is determined by our study and meditation on the Word daily.

F. WHY YOU NEED A CHURCH:

Why You Need a Church Family. A church family identifies you as a genuine believer. I can't claim to be following Christ if I'm not committed to any specific group of disciples. Jesus said, "Your love for one another will prove to the world that you are my disciples." John 13:35 (NLT) When we come together in love as a church family from different backgrounds, race, and social status, it is a powerful witness to the world. Galatians 3:28 (MSG) You are not the Body of Christ on your own. You need others to express that. Together, not separated, we are His Body.

Part "B"

Chapter 22

A. PERFECT PEACE:

Many of us would think that if we fulfill the conditions of Romans 12:1, then everything else would automatically work out. Yet Paul went on to state that we also have to renew our minds. Many of us who have had made genuine commitments to the Lord but haven't renewed our minds through God's Word, have needlessly suffered many problems. If we think on the same things that the world thinks on, we are going to get the same results. If we keep our minds stayed upon God through the study of His Word and fellowship with Him, then we'll have perfect peace (Isaiah 26:3; Proverbs 23:7).

B. THE KEY TO TRANSFORMED LIFE:

And be not conformed to this world: but be ye transformed by the renewing of your mind, that ye may prove what is that good, and acceptable, and perfect, will of God. Romans 12:2: If we think on the same things that the world thinks on, we are going to get the same results.

If we keep our minds stayed on God through the study of His Word and fellowship with Him, then we'll have perfect peace (Isaiah 26:3). It's that simple. Making our thinking line up with God's Word is the key to a transformation life. It is not God's will that we only are changed on the inside. He wants to manifest this salvation in our physical lives also. That takes place through the renewing of our minds.

C. YOU ARE ON THE WINNING SIDE:

And I say also unto you, that you are Peter, and upon this rock, I will build my church, and the gates of hell shall not prevail against it. Matthew 16:18: This statement about the gates of hell not prevailing against us shows that the church is supposed to be on the offensive, not the defensive, in our spiritual warfare. We shouldn't be just trying to hold out behind our own defenses until Jesus comes to rescue us, but we should be pressing the battle to the very gates of hell itself. The devil and his "imps" should retreat and hide behind their walls, not the church.

D. VICTORY OVER THE DEVIL:

Victory in life over the devil doesn't come by trying to cast out some kind of an evil spirit all the time. It comes from getting your mind so filled with the Word of God that your mind will side in with your spirit. And your spirit directed by the Holy Spirit will lead you in all the affairs of life — including out of the traps and snares of the devil. Unless your thinking is transformed, you can think the devil's thoughts and begin acting just like unsaved people do. But Romans 12:2 says that renewing your mind transforms you! That is the way the Bible says you will be transformed, not by trying to cast a devil out of you. (Read Psalm 1:1-3).

E. DON'T GIVE ACCESS TO THE DEVIL:

You are to actively meditate on the Word of God with your mind so your thinking can be changed or transformed (Ps. 1:1-3). Unless your thinking is transformed, you can think the devil's thoughts and begin acting just like unsaved people do. But Romans 12:2 says that renewing your mind transforms you! That is the way the Bible says you will be transformed, not by trying to cast a devil out of you. Much of what is called "demonic" activity is not caused by demons at all. It is actually the fruit of a believer's, renewed mind — thinking and acting as the world does. An renewed mind gives access to the devil because the mind is the doorway through which the devil gains access to people.

F. ACCORDING TO YOUR FAITH, SO BE IT UNTO YOU:

When we begin to learn what has happened to us in the new creation spirit, the effectiveness of our faith will increase proportionally to our knowledge. Jesus said, "According to your faith, so be it unto you (Matthew 9:29b)." If you want to build the highest type of faith, be a faithful person yourself. Believe in your own word. Establish a reputation for truth; then the Word will be that to you in your life. In Philemon 1:6, Paul says That the communication of thy faith may become effectual by the acknowledging of every good thing which is in you in Christ Jesus. Read 3 John 3:2 prayerfully.

PART "C"

❧

CHAPTER 23

VICTORY THROUGH DISAPPOINTMENT
<u>GOD ALSO ANSWERS THROUGH DISAPPOINTMENTS:</u>
Sometimes God would grant you success by allowing ENEMIES into your life! Yes!

You need people who will mock you, so that you can run to God.

You need people who will try to intimidate you, so that you can be courageous.

You need people who will say "NO" so that you can learn how to be independent... I mean how to do it yourself.

You need people who will work towards you losing that job, so that you can start your own big business.

You need people who will sell your "Joseph" so that "he" can get to Egypt.

You need a cruel landlord, so that you won't be too comfortable in someone else's house, then you can build your own house on time.

But sometimes, when we are disappointed and assumed that our prayers were not answered, we feel very bad and we tend to remain on

85

that spot. Not knowing that the end-point of disappointment is the beginning of your accomplishments.

You may remember that many disappointments you had in the past came with blessings.

You cannot see a new open door while you are still putting all your attention, time and energy in trying to force the closed door to open.

And again I say, "No disappointment from God can ever come without an attached blessing." So, when the disappointment comes, thank God for it and tell "HIM" to open your eyes to see the new blessing that He has for you!

To accomplish a great thing in life, sometimes disappointment must come first in order to pave the way for the through.

In order to have a BREAKTHROUGH, something must first have to break!

That is why it is called "Breakthrough."

MOVING FROM MOCKERY TO MIRACLES

Some Christians are easily offended. Sometimes God allows mockery and insults to come our way in order to test our patience and dependence on him. If only we can shun our pride and disallow it from showing up at such testing moments, then it will make room for God to take us to a higher level in him and then be blessed. Our mockeries will then give way for us to receive God's miracles and our insult will guarantee us to get good results of what we need.

In 2 Kings, chapter 5, we read about the captain of the Syrian Army named Naaman, a man of authority and honor, who traveled all the way from Syria to Israel to see Elisha the prophet in order to be cured of his leprosy because he was a leper. On his arriving at Elisha's door with his entourage, Elisha did not even bother to come out of his room to welcome him. Elisha the prophet simply sent his servant to go and tell him to go and wash seven times in the Jordan River. Jordan River was not a clean river when compared to some other rivers in Syria. As Naaman humbled himself and did what the prophet told him to do, he was healed of his leprosy. If he had disobeyed, he would have remained a leper all the days of his life on earth and would have eventually died a leper.

Hannah was a woman in need of a child of her own. In 1 Samuel 1:14, as she was praying for a child in the temple, the Priest in charge addressed her as a drunk. She did not angrily walk away from the temple but took time to explain to the priest Eli that she was not drunk but praying unto God. God eventually granted her the child Samuel. I still remembered an incident that happened in my church many years ago. A grandmother came to the Sunday Service to worship and sat on a back seat reserved for women with kids. One of the ushers gently approached her and demanded if she could move to any of the seats in front of her and reminded her that the seat she is sitting on is reserved for nursing mothers. This grandmother, on hearing it, angrily walked away from the church and never came back to the church. Who knows, that Sunday may have been the very Sunday God would have granted her years of requests from God but she missed the prayer time that would have turned things around in her life.

In Mathew 15:26-28, when a Canaanite woman requested Jesus to heal her sick daughter, Jesus answered her by saying, "It is not meet to take the children's bread and to cast it to dogs." The woman did not complain by saying that Jesus was calling her a dog, but with humility she told him that even dogs can eat the crumbs of bread that fall out of their master's table. Jesus, on hearing the woman answer, commended her by saying, "O woman, great is thy faith." Her sick daughter was eventually healed. If this woman had walked away angrily on hearing the first response of Jesus she would have missed the opportunity of getting her daughter healed miraculously. According to Galatians 5:22, longsuffering is one of the fruits of the Spirit, to receive from God, you must have patience.

Have patience and wait for the thing you want most. Keep praying, and believing God for the answer to come. If God wants you to have it, He will give it to you.

TRIAL BEFORE GOD'S BLESSINGS

Trials can be beneficial. God can use them for our purpose. He makes ALL things work together for our good (Romans 8:28). God does not tempt anyone with evil (James 1:13b).

God can use our trials to bless us if we respond positively and righteously to it. Our trials then become a stepping stone that will pave the way for our blessings. Not all trials are meant to hurt you but to pave way for God's blessings to be manifested in your life. Sometimes, the scripture refers to trials as temptations.

Many times your trials or temptations come through humans like you. As you form the habit of praying without ceasing, God will grant you the power to resist the trials or temptations. The word of God teaches us not to see our trials or temptations as strange but to welcome them with joy. In 1 Peter 4:12, it says: "Beloved, think it not strange concerning the fiery trial which is to try you, as though some strange thing happened unto you." Also, in James 1:2, it says: "My brethren, count it joy when you fall into divers temptations (trial)."

Sometimes, you need people who will mock you, so that you can run to God.

You need people who will try to intimidate you, so that you can be courageous.

You need people who will say "NO" so that you can learn how to be independent… I mean, how to do things on your own.

You need people who will work towards you losing that job, so that you can start your own big business.

You need people who will sell your "Joseph" so that "he" can get to Egypt…Genesis 37:38. If Joseph was not sold to the Egyptians, he would not have been made the second-in- command to the Egyptian king. As the second-in-command in Egypt, Joseph was well positioned to save his family from starvation.

You need a cruel landlord, so that you won't be too comfortable in someone else's house, then you can be motivated or agitated enough to buy or build your own house on time.

But sometimes, when we face trials we feel disappointed and assume that our prayers are not answered, we feel very bad and we tend to remain on that spot. Not knowing that the end-point of our trial or disappointment is the beginning of our accomplishments.

You cannot see a new open door while you are still putting all your attention, time and energy in trying to force the closed door to open.

And again I say, "None of our trials or disappointments, can ever come without an attached blessing." (In Genesis 50:2, Joseph said to his brothers who sold him, that they meant it for evil against him, but God meant it to abundantly bless him. In Job 42:12, after all the trails Job went through, the Lord blessed the latter end of Job more than his beginning.) So, when the trial or disappointment comes, thank God for it and tell "HIM" to open your eyes to see the new blessing that He has for you!

James 1:12: "Blessed is the man that endures temptation (trial): for when he is tried, he shall receive the crown of life, which the Lord had promised to them that love him."

PART "C"

∋⋲

CHAPTER 24

VICTORY THROUGH YOUR FAITH IN GOD
<u>ACCEPT GOD-GIVEN OPPORTUNITIES:</u>
Proverbs 14:12

"There is a way which seems right to a man and appears straight before him, but at the end of it is the way of death."

Many times, opportunities present themselves to us and it's only through the guidance of the Spirit that you can recognize which opportunities are from God. The Bible says there's a way that "seems right" to a man; in other words, it looks like the opportunity is the right one, but the end of it is "the way of death." Notice that it uses the word "ways," not "way." Meaning that as long as a man is on that road, no matter which way he turns, since it's not God leading him, he's certainly going to end up in trouble.

This is why you must learn to recognize and enter only such doors of opportunities opened for you by the Spirit of God. When your church presents you with the opportunity to fast and pray with the rest of other church members, then, through the help of the Spirit you must recognize that it is from God. The devil would not tell you to do what would help you to grow closer to God and be blessed. Natural opportunities that didn't come from God may sometimes be very appealing, but refuse to act on them. It reminds me of what someone said, "If God didn't want me to have that thing, why did He let me get it?" That you got it doesn't mean it's in line with God's perfect will for your life.

This is the dilemma in which many Christians have found themselves. For example, someone might have been working somewhere, and suddenly hears of another job opportunity in a different organization, with better pay, and decides to take it up without asking, "Lord, should I go?" You may be a member of a church and feel that you have discovered some imperfection in the life of one or two members in that church. The Holy Spirit may be directing you to start praying for those imperfect individuals and not to leave that church to another. Leaving the church to another may result in your forfeiting the blessings God intended for you. God doesn't want you to live a life of "trial and error," this is why you need the guidance of the Holy Spirit in your life.

In Genesis 13, we read about Lot, how a natural opportunity presented itself to him when Abraham asked him to choose which way he would like to go. Lot immediately jumped at the opportunity of going to the seemingly flourishing land of Sodom, instead of asking Abraham, the prophet of God, "Which way should I go?" In the end, Abraham ended up a thousand times greater, and eventually inherited even the part Lot had chosen, but Lot lost everything and ended up in a cave (Genesis 19:30).

Although King David was an experience soldier and fighter, he had fought and won so many battles but every time before her goes to battle, he would first inquire of the Lord. David was not counting on his own strength but on the strength of the Lord. He was depending on God's willingness to help him defeat his enemies. 1 Samuel 30:8, and

David inquired of the Lord, "Shall I pursue this…," 2 Samuel 5:19: "So David inquired of the Lord, 'Shall I go and attack….'" It was recorded at least seven times in the Bible that David inquired of the Lord before he went to battle his enemies: 1 Samuel 23:2, 1 Samuel 23:4, 1 Samuel 30:8, 2 Samuel 2:1, 2 Samuel 5:19, 2 Samuel 5:23 and 2 Samuel 21:1.

Embrace God-given opportunities. Make sure you seek for the face of God before you embark on any task. You need God's approval in order to succeed.

Let the Holy Spirit guide you in your choices. Fasting and praying for your church and for yourself is one of the right choices the Holy Spirit will enable you to make at the beginning of a new year. Follow Him; don't go ahead of Him to make your own choice and then ask Him to bless it. Refuse to let your mind not to hear the voice of God in your spirit. No matter what promise of a better life an opportunity dangles in front of your eyes, train yourself to pray and listen to God's voice before you dive at such opportunities. That way, you'll only accept God-given opportunities!

GOD JUDGES YOUR ACTIONS

The blessings or judgments you receive from God are sometimes not directly proportion to your actions in the past. Like the case of a man in the Bible named Job (Job 1:12-22), he was righteous before God, but for reasons best known to the Lord. He allowed Satan to take him through some challenges: He lost his children, houses and good health. After Satan finished tormenting him, God gave him double blessings of what he had before Satan bankrupted him. When God allow you to go through a torment that was not caused by your sins or fault of your own, He will eventually make it up for you.

Sow seeds of good action so that you can eventually reap blessings from God. Gal. 6:9: "And let us not be weary in well doing for in due season we shall reap, if we faint not."

For the type of seed you sow is the same type of fruit you will eventually reap. Now look at the following people in the Bible who sowed different types of seeds in what they said and did and reaped a harvest of like manner. In many cases, God in response to someone's action will openly say to the person, this or that will I do to you for your actions, in other times He would simple go ahead to judge him or her without saying a word.

In 2 Samuel 11:4-17, after King David killed Uriah and took his wife (Bathsheba), God then sent Nathan the prophet to David to tell King David in 2 Samuel 12:12, that <u>because David did this evil, secretly against Uriah the Hittite, that God will do it to David publicly before all Israel, and before the sun.</u>"

In Genesis 22:2, because Abraham obeyed God to offer his only son (Isaac) unto God, in the process of doing just that, God in 2 Samuel 22:16:18 said to him, "<u>because you have done this thing,</u> and has not withheld your son, your only son, I will multiply your children as the stars of the heaven and on you all the nations of the earth shall be blessed."

God may as well judge pride and foolishness. The Scripture teaches in James 4:6 and 1 Peter 5:5 that God resists the proud. In 2 King 20:12-13, when the pagan King of Babylon sent his son and some of his men to visit Hezekiah after his illness, without a second thought, because he wanted to show off his pride, he showed the men from Babylon all the treasure of Israel. Through the mouth of prophet Isaiah, God said to Hezekiah (2 Kings 20:17), "<u>because of what you have done,</u> a day will come when all these treasures you have showed to them in your household shall be carried into Babylon, and nothing shall be left."

In Mark 14:3, a woman came, having an alabaster box of very precious ointment of spikenard, and poured the ointment on Jesus' head. Jesus then answered to one of the disciples, who complained that the action was unnecessary waste of ointment (Mark 14:9), "Verily I say unto you, where-so-ever this gospel shall be preached through the whole world, this also she has done shall be spoken of for a memorial of her."

In 1 Chronicle 13:14, Obed-edom the Gittite housed the ark of God when King David was afraid to bring the ark to Jerusalem. God was very pleased with Obed-edom for this thing he did. God did not say any word to him but went ahead to bless him and his household. Every living creature in his house was blessed.

Finally, God appeared to King Solomon in a dream, telling him to ask for a thing to be given to him (1Kings 3:5). Solomon asked God for wisdom to judge Israel (verse 9). Solomon's request pleased God (verse 10-14). He then said to him, <u>"because you have not asked for long life, riches for yourself or for the life of your enemies but only asked for wisdom, I will go ahead to add these other things which you did not ask for to the wisdom I will give."</u>

As you dedicate yourself in the period of praying and fasting, you can ask the Lord to help you guide your actions toward the things that please Him. And let us not be weary in doing good, for in due season we shall reap, if we faint not (Gal. 6:9). God in turn can say to you, "Because you have obeyed me or have done this or that in my Name, therefore I will do so and so for you!"

PART "C"

CHAPTER 25

VICTORY THROUGH PRAYER

<u>A PERSON OF GOD PRAYS ALWAYS:</u> We read from II Chronicles 7:14 about God saying, "If my people, which are called by my name, shall humble themselves, and pray, and seek my face, and turn from their wicked ways, then will I hear from heaven, and will forgive their sin, and heal their land."

From this passage, there are two main issues at stake here that need to be dealt with. The first one is that the people of God have sinned and needed to be forgiven by God. The second is that because of the sins of the people of God, their land is polluted and sick and need to be healed by God. To resolve this challenge, the people of God need to humble themselves to pray, seeking the face of God, turn from their wicked ways and start doing what is right in the sight of God.

If you are a Christian or a person of God, this word is for you. Are you dealing with an issue, which you have no solution on how to solve it? This word is for you. Pray, I mean, to pray-pray and pray until God

97

changes things. If the power is found to be in the hands of the devil, your prayer will cause power to change hands. People of God know how to cry to God in good time and in time of need because in Psalm 46:1 and Hebrews 4:16, we learn that God is a present help in time of need.

The children of Israel cried out to God (Exodus 3:7) because of punishments from their taskmasters in Egypt, God delivered them by the hands of Moses and brought them, into a good land flowing with milk and honey.

When the Israelites decided to abandon the God that brought them out of the land of slavery in Egypt (Judges, chapter 6 &7) and began to serve Baal, the pagan god, God allowed the Midianites to torment them on a daily basis right in their homeland. Even while they were in sin, they cried unto God and he had mercy and delivered them from the hands of the Midianites. Under the leadership of Gideon, God gave them victory with just 300 men instead of the 22,000 men that Gideon initially assembled to fight the Midianites.

A person of God should know that the most powerful weapon available for all God's children is prayer. Prayer is the most powerful weapon to use to win any spiritual battle.

PRAYER IS A GIFT FROM GOD

There is something about prayer that is very powerful. Prayer is a gift from God._In Matthew 26:41, Jesus told Peter to watch and pray so that he would not enter into temptation. This means that if Peter had prayed (in group with the two sons of Zebedee) he would have averted the temptation of denying Jesus thrice before the cock crowed.

In Ezekiel 22:30: God was looking for a man to stand on the gap and pray so that he would not destroy the land, but found none. That means that your prayer can make a difference. It is capable of preventing God from destroying a city or a nation. God can save nations from impending disasters when we pray!

In Jeremiah 29:7: God told his people to pray for the peace of the city where they were taken into captivity, He told them that when there is peace in that city, they too shall have peace. It shows that your prayer is capable of restoring or enabling a city or nation to remain in peace.

Finally, in 2 Chron.7:14, we read: "If my people, which are called by my name, shall humble themselves, and pray…, then will I hear from heaven, and will forgive their sin, and will heal their land." Here we know that when you pray, God will hear you and forgive you and the people you are praying for. Your prayer is capable of making God to heal your land.

YOU TOO CAN PRAY AND GOD WILL ANSWER YOU

Isaiah 1:8, "Come now, and let us reason together says the Lord." God is willing to hear what you have to say and then answer you back. Every good father is willing to grant audience to any of his children, so is our loving father in heaven. Do you have reason why God should grant you what you are asking for, then tell it to Him.

1 Chronicle 4:10-11: Here we learn that the mother of Jabez gave birth to him in pains and then decided to name him "Jabez," meaning "pain." The significance of this was that Jabez might live all his life suffering in pain and causing pain since he was born in pain.

When Jabez grew up and knew God, he did not like the curse of pain placed on him by his mother. Jabez then prayed unto our loving God, saying, "Oh, that thou would bless me indeed, and that your hand might be with me, and that thou would keep me from evil, that it might not grieve me!" God then granted him his request.

Even today, there are people whose parents had told that they would not amount to anything in life when they were little children. If you are one of those people, you should reject such a curse in Jesus' name. Turn to God and God would do for you what he did for Jabez.

In 2 Kings 20:1-6, God had already sent Amoz his prophet to inform King Hezekiah that he will die in his illness, but Hezekiah decided to negotiate his life with God. He reminded God to consider the good things he had done in his name, so God changed his mind and added another fifteen years to his life on earth.

It is important to note that when Abraham in the book of Genesis 18:25-33 prayed a prayer of negotiation for Sodom and Gomorrah, God did not grant the request because there was nothing to back it up. All the people that lived in Sodom and Gomorrah were deep in sin. Abraham could not find at least ten righteous people, which would have influenced and made God change his justice for their sin.

In 2 Chronicles 20:10-23, King Jehoshaphat reminded God of how Israel showed favor to the nations of Ammon, Moab and Mount Seirs by not invading them when Israel came out of the land of Egypt and was heading to the promised land, but they have now turned against Israel. God then turned these three nations against themselves and they killed one another.

You too can pray a prayer of negotiation if you have good reason to back it up.

CHAPTER 26

VICTORY THROUGH NEGOTIATING WITH GOD

<u>ASK TO RECEIVE:</u> John 14:13: "If you shall ask any thing in my name, I will do it."

Jesus so loves us that He gave us an open invitation to ask God for our needs so that He can grant it to us. Simply because you once asked for a thing and you did not receive it or has not yet received it does not mean that the next time you ask you would not receive. You may not know the circumstances that caused you not receive it or why you have not yet received what you asked for. Unfortunately, some Christians are yet to take advantage of this. Some would say, "I don't like to take God for granted," or "What if I'm being greedy? What if God is not willing to give me what I'm asking for?"

Well, Jesus, in the Scripture above, answered all questions, and clearly reveals that it's the Father's good pleasure to answer your prayers, and to grant your requests so that your joy may be full. Not only is God able, He's equally willing to grant any request you make in the name of Jesus. This is why Jesus said clearly, "Ask and it shall be given you…" (Luke 11:9).

You may be wondering, "How do I know if what I'm asking for is consistent with God's will?" Well, Jesus said, "If ye abide in me, and my words abide in you, ye shall ask what ye will, and it shall be done unto you" (John 15:7). That's your assurance—if you abide in him and His Word abides in you, then your will gets lined up with his will, your desires will be in harmony with his plans and purpose for your life.

Doublemindedness, hesitating and doubts (signs of lack of faith) are hindrances to having your prayers answered. James 1:6 & 7 says that it must be by faith that he asks, with no wavering. For the one who wavers is like the billowing surge out at sea that is blown hither and thither and tossed by the wind. For truly, let no such a person imagine that he will receive anything from the Lord. So, stop doubting!

The Lord doesn't want you sad, bitter or frustrated in life. He wants your joy to be full always. That's why He gave you an open invitation to ask Him anything in faith, and expect to receive answers. Matthew 7:8 says: "For every one that ask, shall receive…." Asking will be incomplete until you have received. So if there's anything you desire right now, put your faith to work! Go ahead and ask the Father in the Name of Jesus, and receive the answer by faith. Sometimes the answer may come immediately and sometimes, God may choose to delay it for reasons best known to Him. Remember that delay does not mean denial.

God is a giver; He gives generously and graciously to all without holding back. (James 1:5).

SOMETHING ABOUT NEGOTIATING WITH GOD

This is to encourage you. There is something about prayer that is very powerful. Prayer is a gift from God.

In Matthew 26:41, Jesus said to Peter to watch and pray that he enter not into temptation. That means that if Peter prays in group with the two sons of Zebedee he would have averted the temptation of denying Jesus thrice before the cock crowed.

In Ezekiel 22:30 God was looking for a man to stand on the gap and pray so that he should not destroy the land, but found none. That means that your prayer can make a different. It is capable of preventing God from destroying a city or a nation.

In Jeremiah 29:7 God said to his people to pray for the peace of the city where they were taken captives, saying that for in the peace of that city, they shall have peace. It shows that your prayer is capable of restoring or enabling a city or nation to remain in peace.

Finally, in 2 Chron.7:14, we read: "If my people, which are called by my name, shall humble themselves, and pray…, then will I hear from heaven, and will forgive their sin, and will heal their land." Here we know that when you pray, God will hear you and forgive you and the people you are praying for. Your prayer is capable of making God to heal your land.

Now that you see what your prayers is capable of doing, why not take the advantage, of creating room, once again of joining us for prayer on the first Saturday (6:00 P.M.) of every month and on every Wednesday (6:30 P.M.) at the church. If you have been coming, keep coming. If you have not been coming, start again to come.

PART "C"

CHAPTER 27

HAVE PATIENCE AND EXPECT VICTORY FROM GOD
<u>GOD IS GREATER AND STRONGER THAN OUR STRANGE ENEMIES</u>: Many Bible-translators translate Ephesians 6:12-13 as: "we wrestle not against flesh and blood but against principalities and powers on high places," but the better translation is "we are not fighting against people but against unseen strange enemies." These strange enemies are the proprietors of many of the strange attacks we face as we walk with the Lord. In the book of Isaiah 28:21, we read that our God also does his strange work and is doing his strange act to bring to nothing the evil works of these strange enemies of his children.

To many Christians, these attacks must have lasted for a very long time. All the prayers may seem not to have removed the problem. The problem may now even seem like an everlasting mountain, the type described in Habakkuk 3:6, which the Lord promised to scatter. It is interesting to note that in Habakkuk 3:10 it is written, the mountains saw the Lord and trembled, showing that even the everlasting mountain must bow to our Lord.

Fasting and aggressive prayers is a very strong weapon against these strange enemies.

Even if the strange enemies pose as giants, they can be defeated. Giants exist to be defeated. David as a young man did not ran away from the Philistine giant who he contended with, rather he ran toward him and cut away his head as it is recorded in 1 Samuel 17:48. It is my prayer that God would grant you victory over any giant and the everlasting mountains in your life in Jesus' name.

OUR GOD GOES THE EXTRA MILE WITH YOU

In Joshua 10:10-12, we read of how five heathen nations came to attack Israel (God's people). They wanted to take Gibeon, which now belongs to Israel. God not only helped his people to defeat them, but as those not killed were trying to flee, God rained large stones to destroy those fleeing. It is my prayer for you that if you are a child of God that God would rain large spiritual stones on all those powers of darkness coming after you, in Jesus' name. In Isaiah 41:11, God promised that those that strive with you shall perish.

Our God is willing to go the extra mile to help his people (his blood-washed children, who love him, obey him, look up to him and trust him).

From the book of Genesis, as Israel traveled from Egypt through the wilderness to their promised land, they met with different obstacles but in each case, God intervened and helped them miraculously. When they came to the Red Sea, the Lord literally made a way in the Red Sea for them to pass through. The Lord repeated this miraculous act again when they came to the Jordan River. When they needed water, the Lord made the rock to produce water for his people to drink. When they were hungry, the Lord rained down heavenly food (Manna) for them to eat. The Lord gave Israel victory over all their enemies who came to attack them. When the walls of Jericho posed as an obstacle, the Lord literally pushed the walls down. Finally, Israel was made to inherit houses they did not built and gardens that they did not plant. Let us diligently look up to him at ALL times.

Isaiah 30:19b tells us that "God will be very gracious to you at the sound of your cry; when He hears it, He will answer you." Have you really cried unto God when you are really in need?

In your last health check, you might have received a bad report from your doctor but God is able to change your story if only you are willing to really pray continuously and to cry unto him.

2Kings 13:14-19, we read that Syria was a sworn enemy to the people of Israel. Joash, the king of Israel, cried to Prophet Elisha for help. The prophet gave him some arrows and ordered him to smite the ground with the arrows. Joash smote the ground three times and stopped but the Prophet became very angry with him, saying that he should have smote the ground up to five or six times before stopping. He made Joash to know that he will be able to defeat Syria only three times but if he had smote the ground five or six times, he would have completely defeated Syria and never would have experience any future treat from that nation. The lesson we can learn from this is that when God tells us to do something, we should do it with all our might. In Joel 3:10b, it reads: "Let the weak say, I am strong." When you are sick and weak, keep telling yourself in faith that you are strong until you find yourself healed and strong again. As a child of God, when you face challenges, do what the word of God instructs us to do. 1Thes. 5:17 says: "Pray without ceasing." In Luke 18:1 Jesus says: "Men ought always to pray, and not to faint." Keep praying until the result comes.

Prayer is a God-given invaluable treasure to man, only those who are convinced of its true value use it most effectively. Prayer is not meant to be a barren exercise but the divine channel to communicate with God.

If you are willing and obey, the Lord is willing to go the extra mile to help you.

WHY ARE YOU WORRIED?

Worry is darkness in a place of uncertainty. In Philippians 4:6-7, God asks us to always bring our anxieties to him. God promised to give us inexplicable peace different from that offered by the world around us. This peace would keep worry away from our hearts and mind. Peace is not the absence of problems but it is going through problems without being disturbed.

Peace is not the absence of trouble. In Luke 12:22-23, God enjoins us to trust him and not to be anxious over our needs because he cares and will supply. We have a physician who can heal where the doctors cannot. God knows what we go through in life and cares. Let us habitually turn our worries over to God.

Someone is still asking God when his debts will be settled! The truth is that the debts started one day, God will also help you to settle it one day if you let him! God has a plan for you and nothing will stop it. God's plan has timing, he knows what he is doing. So, stop worrying!

Worry will make you to forget God's ability and the things he has done. When we worry, we show that we do not trust God's ability to change our unpleasant situations and circumstances.

Troubles and victories are parts of life. How else do you have victory and a testimony without a battle?

In Mark 4:37-40 Jesus was sleeping at the back of the boat with his head on a cushion while a storm tossed their boat about. The disciples woke him up, shouting, "Teacher, don't you care that we're going to drown?" Are you going through a tough time? Are you tossed about by the storms of life? Do you want to shout, like the disciples did in their wave-torn boat, "Don't you care about me at all, God?" Worry means "I don't think God can do it." In verse 39, Jesus got up and rebuked the wind, saying, "Peace be still." Is Jesus in your boat? If Jesus is still in your boat, remember that the winds still obey him. Jesus is saying,

"Peace be still." In Psalm 46 verse 10 he says, "Be still and know that I am God...."

There is absolutely no benefit of feeling worried. God will not be forced to answer your prayers simply because you are worrying, but rather it makes God to feel that you have no faith in him. And sure, research suggests that worrying can cause stress, lead to heart attacks, breakdowns, panic attacks, sometimes you can't think straight and it can potentially lead you to physically being ill.

By prayer and thanksgiving, let your supplications be made known to God. Peace means relax, God is in charge. Take your anxieties to God in prayer and have a good sleep.

❧❧

Chapter 28

AMAZING LIFE'S STORIES OF HOPE

I hope reading this book must have been beneficial to you. You are beginning to see a ray of light towards the end of the channel. For you that may still contemplating to become a Christian, it is may pray that you make a quick decision to become one. You that already a Christian, remember what the Bible says in Romans 8:31, "If God be for us, who can be against us." Even in your Christianity, people can still judge you wrongfully.

A pastor was invited to dinner by a couple in his church. As the couple was sitting near a table where the dinner was served, they discovered a fifty-dollar note on the same table, so the pastor took the fifty-dollar note and put it inside the couple's Bible on a table near the window. The pastor noticed after that visit, that the couple did no more come to his church for six months until he met the couple at a shopping store. As the pastor question the couple as to why they have been absent from the church, they complained that they were offended because the pastor took their fifty-dollar note on their table, the day he visited them. The pastor then replied to them by saying that he put the fifty dollar note in their Bible on the table near to the window, because he did not was source from the food to spill on the fifty-dollar note. It shows that the couple did not even read or open their Bible for six months, that is the reason, why they did not find the fifty-dollar note.

The former President of America, Franklin D. Roosevelt was complaining that people were miss-quoting him and were not listening to him whenever he is speaking. One day during an event he decided to prove himself right. As people file on line to see him, he would say to each person: "I murdered my grandmother this morning." Each of the visitor would respond, "Mr. President I came to thank you for all your good works, continue your good works for our country." It was until the 10th visitor, who was the Bolivian President, who came to shake his hand and he said to him, "I murdered my grandmother this morning", who then responded "What a sad news to hear, I hope you handle this matter very well."

A little girl was given two apples by one of her uncles. Her mother requested one of the apples from the little girl. The little girl, instead of just giving one of the apples to her mother, simple tested or bit the two apples. The mother almost became offended and wanted to walk away from her, but the little girl suddenly showing one of the apples to her mother, said "Mommy, take this apple, it tests better than the other." It was then the mother realized that her daughter wanted to make sure she gives her Mommy the apple that test better.

In our walk in life, sometimes we blame others falsely. An old man kept telling her old wife the she had a hearing problem, but his wife kept telling him that there is no problem with her ears. One morning, as the wife was sitting facing their kitchen window, her husband decided to prove to his wife that she has a hearing problem. He slicked behind his wife and said "can you hear me now?" The man did not hear any respond from his wife. The man repeated the same question for the fourth times. It was at the fourth times that the wife turned around to face her husband and said, "For this fourth times, you have asked me the same question, saying 'can you hear me now' and each time, I have always answered you saying 'I can hear you'. What is wrong with you? It seems you have hearing problem; you need to see a doctor.' It was only then the old man realized that he is the one having hearing problem and not his old wife.

Sometimes in life, people say things or act in certain ways to display what they are not really are. A former British Prime Minister, Winston Churchill was going to BBC in London to make a speech to his country. In those days, there were no security to protect the leaders of States as we have it now. So, he hired a taxi to take him to BBC London. The taxi driver did not know that he was the Prime Minister Britain. On getting to the BBC premises, Churchill instead of giving the taxi driver the one pounds he promised him, gave him five pounds and asked the driver to wait for him for the next forty-five minutes because he had an appointment at the office in the BBC building. The taxi driver objected, saying that he was hurrying home to listen to the Prime Minister speech over the BBC. The prime Minister was impressed that this taxi driver was very much interested to go home to listen to what he has to say to the nation of Britain. The Prime Minister then decided to reward the taxi driver with twenty pounds. The taxi driver on receiving the twenty pound from the Prime Minister, said to him, You can take all the time you want, I will wait for you even for the whole day. The Prime Minister then said to the taxi driver, "Are you no longer going to listen to the Prime Ministers speech." The taxi driver then replied, "With this amount of money you gave me, I do not care of whatever the Prime Minister have to say."

People may not welcome your good intention for them, but you should not allow it to discourage you in your good works. Amaira was an Indian lady who had a hunchback. She was of the Buddha religion. One day one of her neighbor who was a Christian, invited her to a Christian crusade, hoping that Jesus would heal her of her hunchback. At the crusade ground, Amaira was healed. She became so excited and decided to invite some of her friends who were of the Buddha religion to her house to hear her testimony of how Jesus healed her of her hunchback. When her friends arrived at her house, she informed them that he is now a Christian, that Jesus healed her of her hunchback in a Christian crusade. One of her friends she invited, ten said to her, "Amaira, it is better that you are not healed of your hunchback and re-main a Buddha than to become a Christian." Amaira replied her saying that Buddha did not heal her all these years of her hunchback, that her friend can now have her hunchback, that henceforth she will be follow-ing Jesus who has healed her. He finally said that Buddha did not heal her and that it is Jesus who healed her, that henceforth she will be fol-lowing Jesus who healed her.

You should not allow things or people to determine whether you should be happy or not. Let no one rub you of your joy. A story was told about a village in Africa. The people in this village had a traditional believe that a man can determine how his day will be, depending on which side his coin will turn when he flips it. Every morning, when a man wakes up, he would flip a coin. If when he flips the coin, and the tail was facing up, the man will assume that he was going to have a bad day; But, if when he flips the coin, and the head was facing up, the man will assume that he was going to have a good day. He would go ahead rejoicing, believing that he was going to be a happy man all the day. In that same village a group men noticed that there was a particular man who was always happy, day in and day out. They wonder among them-selves, "Why is this man coin always turning to the head side, whenever he flips it." The men then decided visit the man to tell them his secret. On arrival at the man's house, he explained to them that he had decided not to allow an object like the coin to rub him of his joy. He said that he believes in the tradition of flipping the coin every morning when he gets up. That whenever he flips the coin and it turns to the head side facing up, he would go his day business knowing that he is going to have a good day; But if when he flips his coin and it turns to turns to the tail side facing up, then he would use his hand to turn the coin to make the head side facing up. He concluded by saying that in this way, my coin was always having the head side facing up. That was the reason he was always happy and having good days.

Jesus on one of his teaching about the kingdom of heaven, used little children in his illustration. Quoting from Matthew 18:3 says, "Unless you become like little children, you will never enter the kingdom of God." Little children are direct and honest and say things the way they see it. My wife has a little niece of about 5 years old, one day this her niece saw a lady sitting in the living area waiting for her uncle Mike who has gone few minutes earlier. Her uncle mike was the type that is known for flirting with different ladies. So the 5 years old child just went directly to the lady sitting in the living room, waiting for her uncle Mike and said to her, "Why are you waiting here, uncle Mike will not marry you. He has many girl-friends." Another lady once came to visit her uncle Mike. As soon as the 5 years old child saw that her uncle Mike went into the bathroom, she quickly went and stand facing the visiting lady. The lady said to her, "little girl. Why are you looking at me, do you like my beautiful face or my beautiful dressing?" The 5 years old, simply nodded in disapproval and said, Rabbit nose, you have a rabbit nose."

A man owed another man the sum of eight hundred dollars. One morning, the man he borrowed the money from called to say that he will be coming at 2:00pm that afternoon to collect his eight hundred he borrowed from him. The man who borrowed the money, seeing that he has not the money to refund to the other man, decided to deceive the man he borrowed money from. He instructed his 4 years old child to tell the man who will be coming to their home at 2:00pm that he is not home. When this other man arrived at the home he rang the bell to the home. The little 4 years old child looked out of the window and said to him, "My father said that I should tell you that he is not home." The man ten responded by asking him, "But where is he?" The little 4 years old child answered by saying, "He is sleeping in the bedroom."

It is said that honesty is the best policy. It is sad to see that not everyone wants to hear the truth. A young man once informed his mother that he was going to marry and wed his long time girl-friend, Elizabeth. The mother objected to it, saying the she was not the right woman for him. The young man persisted that she had known her for years and that he feels comfortable marrying her. The young man's mother insisted that her son should make her a promise that if he marry her, that he will never bring her to her mother's house. The young man agrees and went ahead, married his long time girl-friend, Elizabeth. After the marriage, as years passed by, Elizabeth started questioning her husband as to while he refused to take her to visit her husband's mother. The husband who had grown tired of making excuses to his wife, simple answered to his wife by saying, "My mother said that she could not stand you, and that she hated the way you always roll your eyes."

An 85 years old woman was visiting a zoo in south Africa where he saw a chimpanzee sitting on a commode, having a news-paper in it hands, upside down, pretending to be reading the news-paper. The old woman passed by but later return back to the chimpanzee, looked directly to it face and said, "Don't just sit there, do something."

There are many people who have the wrong idea about God, death, hell and heaven. An 8 years old boy had a mother who is a Christian and a father who was an alcoholic. Whenever he is drunk, he will beat up his wife and son. One day the boy asked her Christian mother saying, "Mother, where do we come from." Her mother answered him saying that we come from God. The boy then said, "Why did daddy said that we come from monkey." The mother replied saying, "Your daddy was only telling you where he comes from, the rest of us come from God. Don't you see the way he always beat bus up whenever he is drunk, it is because he came from monkey."

A man, before he died begged his family to write on his tomb stone, "All dressed up, but no-where to go." A twelve years old boy visiting the cemetery with his Christian family, saw this inscription. He took the marker pen in his pocket, went directly to the tomb stone and wrote, "There is a place to go. You either go to heaven or to hell."

In Galatians 6:7, The Bible teaches that a man reaps what he sows. A couple were having some differences in their marriage stopped talking to each other. The man had a work interview the next day. Since the wife always gets up in the morning at 6:00am to go to her work. When he saw that his wife had gone to the bathroom, he quickly wrote a note telling his wife to wake him at 6:00am when she normally wakes up for work. He did not want to speak to the wife directly because they have not been talking to each other. When his wife woke up the next day at the usual 6:00am, but before she left for work, she simply wrote a note on a piece of paper, placed it near the pillow where her husband was sleeping, saying, "Wake up, it is 6:00am." The husband ended up, waking up at 8:00am, and have to drive for another 45 minutes for an interview that is supposed to start at 8:00am.

The word of God teaches in Ephesians 5:16, that we should redeem the time, because the days are evil. We use our time wisely no matter where we find ourselves, especially when we go to church. A lady learnt her lesson in a hard way in a church. She was sitting inside the church one Sunday, when the pastor was preaching a sermon on why couples should be faithful to their spouses. The lady fell asleep throughout the sermon. Towards the end of the sermon, the pastor spoke with a loud voice, saying, "If you know that you have been cheating in your marriage, stand up." This lady who has been sleeping during preaching of the sermon, suddenly heard only the word "stand-up" and then jumped up on her feet. Although see looked around and was surprise that she was the only one standing up. The pastor then said to her, "Thank you dear lady for standing up and been honest." He then asked her to come forward so he can pray for her. It was after the church service, when some of her friends came to comfort her, that she realized the big mistake she has made. She mistakenly admitted before the congregation the sin she did not commit.

Christians bears good fruits but bad Christians bears bad fruits. Jesus in one of his teachings in Matthew 7:17, says "Every good tree bears good fruit but a bad tree bears bad fruit." A sixteen years old boy ask the father the question on how to know if a person is good or bad. The father took an orange and gave it to his son and asked him to squeeze it. After the son did, orange juice came out of it. The father then said to him, "What came out when you squeezed the orange?" The son answered, "Orange juice." The father again took a tomatoes ball and gave it to his son and asked him to squeeze it like the orange. After the son did, tomatoes juice came out of it. The father then said to him, once again, "What came out when you squeezed the tomatoes ball?" The son answered, "Tomatoes juice." The father then said to his son, "You know if a person is a bad person or a good person by what comes out of that person when squeezed. If when a man is squeezed, bitterness, cursing, hatred and forgiveness comes out of him, then know that he is a bad man; But if a man is squeezed, love, peace and forgiveness still comes out of him, then know for sure that he is a good man.

As good Christians, we should be patient with all people. We must remember that not all people knows what they are doing or saying. A nurse was sent from a Nursing company to the home of a 90 years old woman who had dementia, mental health disorder. On arriving at the woman's home, the dementia woman, called the police saying that a thief had just walked into her room. When the police men arrived at the dementia woman's home, the woman started asking them, why they are here. They police men responded to her, saying that she called them. The old woman then said to the police men, that they were telling lies that she never called them.

In another incident, an 85 years old lady was living with her forty-five years old daughter in the same apartment. One day, the old woman felt offended by her 45 years old daughter and said to her, "I want to die, I do not feel like living anymore." That same evening, the old woman was sitting on a chair, looking outside, from their kitchen window. Her 45 years old daughter, quietly walked close to her and touched her back. The old woman jumped up and screamed, "Stop sneaking on me, you scare me to death."

After the second world war Germany was divided between East and west by the Berlin wall. It was said that there was a time when some men from East Germany took a truck load of garbage and dumped it on the western side of the Berlin wall. In respond, some men from East Germany, took a truck load of groceries and dumped it on the Eastern side of the Berlin wall, with a note attached to the groceries that says, "Let each one gives what he has." In your walk as a Christian, I encourage you to have the mind to forgive others instead of having the mind of un-forgiveness, to love instead of hate, to encourage others instead of looking down on them and to help build others instead of tearing them down.

Talking about social injustice, it is written in Psalm 147:7, that God will executes justice for the oppressed. This is to say that God love justice but hates injustice. Although is written in Deuteronomy 4:31 that "For the Lord your God is a merciful God." But we cannot take the mercy of God for granted and start living like the devil. My two older brothers told me a story of how they tried to take advantage of my Daddy's love and generosity when they were in the junior high school. They said that, once a week they would lie to my Dad that their teacher wanted them to bring money to school. My Dad would give them the money without asking question. My two older brothers would use the money to buy whatever they like when they got to school.

One day, this my two older brothers decided to increase the money they always asked from my Dad, five times more. They lied that it was the teacher who wanted them to bring more money because it would be used for a project in the school. It was at this point that my Dad said to them, "I will be coming to your school to personally hand the money over to your head master and will ask him what he was doing with all the money one of his teacher has been asking them to bring." My two older brothers then realized that they were in in big trouble for lying to my dad, decided to confess that they have been lying and begged my dad not to come to their school to see their head master. My dad then said to them, that all the time they have been telling him that their teacher wanted them to bring money, that he knew that they were lying. Although he had always given them the money any way but as soon as they became greedy and wanted more, so he decided to make them know that he knew that they have been lying to him. Simply because God did not instantly punish a man for sinning should not mean that God will not judge that man if he continues to sin. Just like every other sin, social injustice is a sin and should be avoided.

As Christians, racism and social injustice should not be named among you. It is written in Ephesians 5:3 "And do not let sexual immorality or any impurity (such as racism and social injustice), or greed be named among you." Be determine to say yes to Jesus as the little boy who was asked to play the part of the Inn keeper who refused to give room to Mary and Joseph, for Mary to deliver baby Jesus. This was in a Nativity play during a Christmas pageant in a Church. During the rehearsal of the play, the little boy had protested to his Sunday school teacher, saying that he did not want to play the part of the Inn keeper who said no to Jesus. The Sunday school teacher persisted that he should still be the one to play that part of the Inn keeper. At the day of the play, the little boy stood at the door of the Inn waiting for the arrival of pregnant Mary and Joseph with her. As soon as they arrived at the gate of the Inn, they asked the little boy who is the Inn keeper, to give they a room where Mary can deliver her baby. The little boy, instead of saying that there was no room available in the Inn, instead said: "Yes, there is room, come in to deliver baby Jesus." The audience on hearing this busted laughing and applauding the little boy.

As Christians listen's and sees all the crises, the violence's, the killings and all the turmoil going on in the world today, remember the teachings and assurance from our Lord Jesus in John 16:33: "I have told you these things, so that in me you may have peace. In this world you will have trouble. But take heart, I have overcome the world." The Lord also said in Matthew 18:3, "Except you be converted, and become as little children, you shall not enter the kingdom of heaven." In today's troubled world, Christians should have the altitude of a one 6 years old boy. The little boy was once in a train couch, playing with his toys. The father of this little boy was the driver or operator of the train he was traveling with. All of a sudden, the train started speeding and shaking abnormally. All the adults in the couch, stood up in fear when they noticed how the train was shaking. Few minutes later, everything returned to normal because the train reduced it speed and it was no longer shaking. All the passengers sat back on their seats.

One of the men in the train, noticed that the little was busy playing with his toys throughout the time the train was speeding and shaking abnormally. The man then asked the little boy: "How come you were not afraid when the train was shaking?" The little 6 years old boy simple answered him and said: "The driver of this train is my father, he knows

I am here." The little boy confident was the fact that he knew that his father will not allow anything to happen to him while he was in the train no matter how the train was speeding and shaking. As long as God is in control, there is hope for all who put their trust on him.

The Christians should also know that no matter the crises, the violence's the killings and all the turmoil going on in the world today, God will defend his own.

The word of God says in Philippians 2:4, "Let each of you look not only to his own interests, but also to the interest of others."

A professor gave a balloon to every student, who had to inflate it, write their name on it and throw it in the hallway. The professor then mixed all the balloons. The students were then given 5 minutes to find their own balloon. Despite a hectic search, no one found their balloon.

At that point, the professor told the students to take the first balloon that they found and hand it to the person whose name was written on it. Within 5 minutes, everyone had their own balloon.

The professor said to the students: "These balloons are like happiness. We will never find it if everyone is looking for their own. But if we care about other people's happiness, well find ours too.

We also read 1 Peter 5:7 "Cast all your anxiety on him because he cares for you. A stressed man was in his office thinking deeply. when suddenly one man ran inside his office, shouting, "Paul, Paul, Paul your daughter Swanta just had an accident and died."

Shocked and confused, he jumped out of his office through the window. As soon as he did, he remembered his office is on the 7th floor.

And, as he descends lower, he remembered he doesn't have a daughter called Swanta.

Still descending, he remembered he is not even married.

Then, just two floors before he hits the ground, he remembered his name is not Paul.

The mercy of God saved him, he fell on a Lorry carrying foams. As long as God is in control, there is hope for all who put their trust on him.

In the mist of social injustice, hatred and un-forgiveness, there still others who believe that humanity has not lost integrity and the ability to fulfill promises made. and has not lost the will to do good to others."

During the reign of an African King named Eze Iheomadiniru, three persons came to him dragging a young man with them and said to him, "Eze Iheomadiniru, this man has murdered our father."

Eze Iheomadiniru: "Why did you kill their father?"

Okorobia: "I'm a shepherd. My sheep ate from their father's farm and he threw a stone at my sheep and it died so I also took the stone and threw it at their father and he also died."

Eze Iheomadiniru: "Because of this, I pass judgment on your charge of murder by sentencing you to death."

Okorobia said:

"I ask for 3 days before you execute the judgment. My late father left me some wealth and I have a sister to take care of. If you kill me now, the wealth and my sister will have no guardian."

Eze Iheomadiniru: "Who will stand for your bail?"

Okorobia looking into the crowd, pointed at Nwankwo.

Eze Iheomadiniru: "Do you agree to stand for him, Nwankwo?"

Nwankwo: "Yes."

Eze Iheomadiniru enquired further: "You agree to stand for someone you don't know and if he doesn't return you'll receive his penalty."

Nwankwo: "I accept."

Okorobia then left but after two days and into the third day there was still no sign of him.

Everyone was very afraid for Nwankwo who had accepted to receive the penalty of death if the man failed to return.

Just before it was time for dinner, the shepherd appeared looking very exhausted and stood before Eze Iheomadiniru.

Okorobia: "I have handed the wealth and the welfare of my sister to my uncle and I am back to receive the penalty. You may execute the penalty now."

In great shock and surprise, Eze Iheomadiniru said: "why did you willingly return after having a chance to escape the death penalty?"

Okorobia: "I was afraid it will appear that humanity has lost integrity and the ability to fulfill promises made."

Eze Iheomadiniru turned and looked at Nwankwo and asked him: "And why did you stand for him?"

Nwankwo responded: "I was afraid it might appear that humanity has lost the will to do good to others."

These words and events moved the brothers who had wanted justice for their father's death very deeply and they decided to forgive the young shepherd.

In anger, Eze Iheomadiniru asked "Why?"

They said: "We are afraid it will appear as though forgiveness has lost place in the heart of humanity."

God is never too early or too late. A young man was getting ready to graduate from college. For many months he had admired a beautiful sports car in a dealer's showroom, and knowing his father could well afford it, he told him that was all he wanted. As Graduation Day approached, the young man awaited signs that his father had purchased the car. Finally, on the morning of his graduation, his father called him into his private study, told him how proud he was to have such a fine son, and how much he loved him. He handed him a beautifully wrapped gift box. Curious, but somewhat disappointed, the young man opened the box and found a lovely, leather-bound Bible, with his name embossed in gold. Angrily, he raised his voice to his father and said, "With all your money you give me a Bible?" He stormed out of the house, leaving the Bible behind.

Many years passed and the young man was very successful in business. He had a beautiful home and wonderful family, but realized his father was very old. He thought perhaps he should go to him. He had not seen him since that graduation day. But before he could make arrangements, he received a telegram telling him his father had passed away, and willed all of his possessions to him. He needed to come home immediately and take care of things. When he arrived at his father's house, sadness and regret filled his heart. He began to search through his father's important documents and saw the Bible as new, just as he had left it years ago. With tears, he opened the Bible and began to turn the pages. His father had carefully underlined a verse, Matt 7:11, "And if ye, being evil, know how to give good gifts to your children, how much more shall your Heavenly Father which is in Heaven, gives to those who ask Him?" As he read those words, a car key dropped from the back of the Bible. It had a tag with the dealer's name, the same dealer who had the sports car he had desired. On the tag was the date of his graduation, and the words... PAID IN FULL. How many times do we miss God's blessings because he did not answer to us the way we expected?

Do not be selfish with all that God has given you.

Even your 10% giving is the acknowledgment that all you have are from God. One day, a very wealthy man was walking on the road. Along the way, he saw a beggar on the sidewalk. The rich man looks kindly on the beggar and asked: "How did you become a beggar?"

The beggar replied, "Sir, I've been applying for a job for a year now but haven't found any. You look like a rich man, Sir, if you'll give me a job, I'll stop begging."

The rich man smiled and said, "I want to help you. But I won't give you a job, I'll do something better. I want you to be my business partner. Let's start a business together."

The beggar blinked hard. He didn't understand what the older man was saying. What do you mean, Sir?"

"I own a rice plantation, said the older man, you could sell my rice in the market. I'll provide you the sacks of rice. I'll pay the rent for the market stall. I'll even give you food allowance, every day, for the next 30 days. All you have to do is sell my rice. And at the end of the month, as *Business Partners*, we'll share in the profits."

Tears of joy rolled down his cheeks. "Oh Sir," he said, "You're a gift from Heaven. You're the answer to my prayers. Thank you, thank you, thank you!"

He then paused and asked, "Sir, how will we divide the profits? Do I keep 10% and give you the 90%? Do I keep 5% and give you the 95%? I'll be happy with any arrangement."

The rich man shook his head and chuckled. "No, I want you to give me the 10% and keep the 90%."

For a moment, the beggar couldn't speak. When he tried to speak, it was gibberish. "Uh, gee, uh, wow, I mean, huh?" He couldn't believe his ears. The deal was too preposterous.

The rich man laughed more loudly. He explained, "I don't need the money, my friend. I'm already wealthy beyond what you can ever imagine. I want you to give me 10% of your profits so you grow in faithfulness and gratitude."

The beggar knelt down before his benefactor and said, "Yes Sir, I will do as you say. Even now, I'm so grateful for what you've done for me!"

Each day, the beggar, now dressed a little bit better, operated a store selling rice in the market. He worked very hard. He woke up early in the morning and slept late at night. And sales were brisk, also because the rice was of good quality, and after 30 days, the profits were astounding.

At the end of the month, as the ex-beggar was counting the money, and liking very much the feeling of money in his hands, an idea grew in his mind. He told himself, "Gee, why should I give 10% to my Business Partner? I didn't see him the whole month! I was the only one who was working day and night for this business. I did all this work! I deserve the 100% profits!"

A few minutes later, the rich man was knocking on the door to collect his 10% of the profits. The ex-beggar opened the door and said, "You don't deserve the 10%. I worked hard for this. I deserve all of it!". Leave me alone, and he slammed the door.

God gave us everything. He gave us life, every single moment, every single breath, every single second. God gave us talents, our ability to talk, to create, to earn money. God gave us our body, our eyes, our ears, our mouth, our hands, our feet, our hearts, HE gave us our mind, our imagination, our emotions, our reasoning, our language. God gave us opportunities, put us in positions, and gave us all we have to make the wealth.

YET we take all of it for granted walking on the earth with pride as if we are self-made? We forget His immeasurable bounties and goodies, and become ungrateful using the very same blessings He gave us to sin and throw back at Him.

Christians are encouraged in the book of James 4:7, to resist the devil and he will flee from you. You should resist the devil because he is not your friend but your enemy. A story was told of a horse that was tied to a tree. A demon came and released him. The horse entered the garden of neighboring peasants and started eating everything. The wife of the owner of the vegetable garden, when she saw this, took a rifle and killed the horse. The owner of the horse saw the dead horse, he became angry, he also took his rifle and shot the farmer's wife. On returning home, the farmer found his wife dead and killed the owner of the horse. The children of the owner of the horse, seeing their dead father, burned the farm of the farmer. The peasant, in retaliation, killed them all. They asked the devil what he had done, and he replied: I did not do anything. I just released the poor horse who was hungry. The devil does simple things ... because he knows that with anger in the heart, wicked desires do the rest. So we must always think before taking any act. Above all, avoid revenge. Wishing evil against others, wanting to solve evil with evil, etc.

You never know the real reasons that lead some people to do certain things, we must take care of our hearts, give ourselves patience and let the storm of anger pass. Because for the demon, just let go of the horse. That horse can be your son, wife, husband, daughter, father, mother, sister, brother, boss, colleague, friend... You have to be matured to really interpret life. Be careful not to let the devil manipulate you! "May GOD guide us every day in life".

Many traditional African quotes can be said to have Biblical significant. Many of the African sayings are quotes of wisdom. The Africa saying that "it takes a village to raise a child" is a quote of wisdom. In Galatians 6:2, says: "Carry each other's burdens and so you will fulfill the law of Christ." In a traditional African village, every village member assumes the responsibility of being a part in the up bring of any child born in that village. A man may not be the father or uncle of a child, but if he sees that child misbehaving or doing what he supposed not to do, the man can step to correct that child not minding who are the parents of that child. The opposite is what we find in the western countries. A man could be sued at the court of law for interfering in the affairs of a child that does not belong to him.

A man's sayings, is an open door to know what he believes in his heart. It means that what a man says is really what he has in his heart.

"If you can no longer swing your arms, fold them on your head." This saying means that you should discard the thing you once have, that have been useful to you but has now become useless. In 2 Corinthians 5:17, says: "Therefore, if any man be in Christ, he is a new creature: old things are become new." You must learn to face reality in life.

The African toad does not run in the day light except something is after its life. In Proverbs 28:1 says: "The wicked flee when no one pursues; But the righteous are as bold as a lion."

"The day you start mocking yourself, others will join you. In Matthew 9:29 says: "According to your faith, be it done unto you." You should be the first to encourage yourself no matter the challenges you face in life. A king in the Bible said when faced enemies coming after him, "I will encourage myself in the Lord, 1 Samuel 30:6." When you keep complaining and mocking yourself, others will support you by joining to mock you as well. To mock yourself is to be like some weak orphan whose precious snack had been wantonly snatched by the village bully.

"A kite that is always scared of chickens has no right or claim to that name." It is not a good idea to name your dog, Lion, if your dog is always scared of people and cats. In 2 Timothy 1:7 says: "For God has not given us the spirit of fear; but of power, of love, and of a sound mind."

Ships don't sink because of the water around them; ships sink because of the water that get into them. In Romans 12:21 say: "Be not overcome of evil, but overcome evil with good." Don't let what's happening around you get inside you and weigh you down.

In 1 Timothy 2:5 says: "For there is one God, and one mediator between God and men, Christ Jesus." The moment the masquerade begins to think he is God, the masquerade will be unmasked and reduced to be a laughing-stock that is lower than a human being." For no man or spirit can assume the position of God. To unmask the African masquerade is to destroy his presumed power or greatness. Let us not forget the fact that behind the guttural mask is a human. The masked one who whips the crowed beyond the borders of entertainment will soon become human once again. Apart from God, humans and things around us are always changing. A man may be up today and may be down tomorrow. No condition is permanent in life. Only God changes not.

Never you think that a person has gone too far and never could be reached with the gospel of Jesus Christ. St Paul in the Bible was once, persecuting the Church until he was dramatically converted to Christianity. Many years ago, I worked with a 60 years old man in an architectural design office. This man hated anything to do with Christianity. One day, he received a call from his son in the American army serving in Afghanistan, saying that he was hearing strange voice, telling him to kill himself and that he feels like committing suicide. The 60 years old man on hearing this from his son, started calling military and government officials, trying to get help for his son, but with no success. The man knowing that I am a Christian then turned to me as his last option, asking me for any possible help or suggestion. I then said to him that I will pray for his son, so he that he will not to kill himself. He answered and said: "Please do." I then went ahead and prayed for his son. Few days later, the 60 years old man, received a call from his son that he has been given permission to travel back to America. On his return to America, he was able to receive cancelling and became normal once again. His son has now been discharge from the army, married, found a good job and living a normal life.

The word of God warned the Christian not to toil with sin. In Numbers 32:23 says: "Be sure your sin will find you out."

Three University guys dodged exam because they did not study.

They came up with a plan, got themselves dirty using grease, then went to see their Lecturer who is a Professor.

"Professor, we are sorry we couldn't make it to the exam. We attended a wedding and on our way back the car broke down thus we became so dirty as you can see". The Professor understood and gave them 3 days to prepare.

After 3 days, they went to the Professor very ready for the exam because they had studied.

The Professor put them in three separate class rooms and gave them the main exam questions that make up 50% of the total mark; and another four questions that make up 50% of the total mark. The following were the other four questions

1. Who got married?
    (25 marks)

2. Where was the reception held?
    (25 marks)

3. Where exactly did the car break down?
    (25 marks)

4. What type of car broke down?
    (25 marks)

Such will be the scenario of the judgment day; we can plan evil with others as a group but on the judgment day we must answer individually for ourselves. Only the truth shall set you free.

Christians should know that the devil is relentless in its effort to defeat us. It should be defeated at all cost. In 1 Peter 5:8 says "Be sober, be vigilant; because your adversary the devil walks about like a roaring lion, seeking whom he may devour." The devil behaves like the birds that goes to eat up the crops which my friend planted in his garden. My friend Willy, likes to make garden on a little piece of land near his house. At the beginning of each year he would plant his favorite crops on his garden, but each time, the birds would go and eat up his crops before they are due for harvesting.

One year, my friend decided to seek a garden expert advice on how to keep the birds away from his garden. The experts advised him to buy an owl figurine and to place it in the center of his garden. This he did and it actually kept the birds away from my friend's garden for a period of time. Whenever the birds see the owl figurine at my friend's garden, they would fly away thinking that it was a real owl. As time goes on, the birds noticed that the suspected owl was always on one spot at the garden and was always motionless. One of the birds decided to go closer to the suspected owl and discovered that it was not lively. So it then perched on the head of the suspected owl but still the owl remained dormant. Then, from that moment on, all the birds returned to my friend's garden and continued eating up its crops. Now, any of the birds that arrives at my friend's garden would first of all perch on the owl figurine's head to pass droppings.

In conclusion, let us again look ones more on the issue of racism and social injustice in our human society. False judgement and wrong thinking towards other people of different race is one of the main cause of racism and social injustice. It is wrong to say that a race is more superior to the other race. People no longer TRUST one another. Where there is no trust, FEAR of the unknown emerges. People usually hate what they fear, and would demonize what scares them. They shut down and shut out any good information that might have help them to see the good sides of people of other race. This FEAR is like a monster living among us that comes out with guns blazing. Fear feeds on a belief in separation and scarcity; separation from what is true, real and uniting and the scarcity of resources and love. Fear talks a language of 'them' and 'us' yours and mine. The language of fear is the language of desperation. Racism and social injustice are the symptoms of a disease; we are all vulnerable to fear. There is only one antidote to fear and that is hope in God combined with love and unity.

If you are not comfortable with the social unrest we see in our society today, then you should join in the fight against racism and social injustice. It is not just enough to talk about it and do nothing. America is a nuclear-armed State with sophisticated weapons, capable of taking their enemies. On the American currency, it is written, "In God we trust." It is not because America don't trust God for protection, but America know that God will not do their own duties. If you want God to keep you healthy, start eating healthy food and be exercising. In proverbs 18:24

says, "If you want to have friends, show yourself friendly." If you want to be a doctor, start studying books on medicine and enroll into a medical school. If you want social justice, fight for justice.

Many have discriminated against people that were divinely placed and orchestrated to help them fulfil their destiny. Some people are un aware when they discriminate against their destiny helpers. A man in Texas learnt this lesson in a hard way years ago when his house was on fire. This white man hated black people and would never have anything to do with them. One afternoon, he was at home sleeping and his house was on fire. A black man happens to be driving through the road where his house was located, saw the burning house, stopped and run into the house to pull out the white man who was still sleeping on his bed. The house was completely burnt down few minutes after the man was pulled out, before the fire fighters arrived at the scene. As this white man re- alized that it was the black man that saved his life, he vowed never to discriminate against any people, no matter their race.

Let us tell it as it is: "Racism and social injustice is bad." The truth will always remain the truth. Learn to say the truth all the time. Jesus did not hide the truth from a man called Nicodemus. He said to him in John 3:3, "Except a man be born again, he cannot see the kingdom of God." A story was told about a woman who had a sick cat. One morn- ing, before the woman left for work, she asked her husband to keep his eyes on her sick cat. At the woman's lunch break, she called her husband who was at home that day, to find out how her sick cat was doing. Her husband simply replied her by saying that her sick cat has died. The woman on hearing that her sick cat has died, screamed very loud over the phone. When she arrived home after work, she blamed her husband for breaking her heart in the way he informed her about the death of her cat. She said that when she called him from work, her husband should have been sensitive to say that her sick cat refused to eat and should have waited to tell her that the cat was dead when she arrived home from work; Saying that in this way, she would not have been badly hurt when he informed her that her sick cat was dead over the phone. The husband then apologized to his wife.

A Christian should always shine the light of his faith, he should not be meddling with the wrong practice of racism and social injustice, because it is as evil as fornication and all types of uncleanness. In Ephesians 5:3 says, "But fornication, and all uncleanness, or covetousness, let it not be once among you..." Christians should position themselves so as to receive the favor of God like a Christian named Peter who went to a job interview.

Peter had a job interview to attend at 10am but his pregnant wife developed complications at 9am. He decided to take the wife to the hospital and leave for the interview thereafter but on their way to the hospital, the taxi broke down. It was already 10:30am before he could get another taxi.

He arrived the hospital at 11am, dropped the wife and used the same taxi to go for the interview. He arrived the interview venue at 12noon (2hours late).

He rang the bell but no one opened the door. Meanwhile, earlier at 10am, the company mail delivery had rung the bell but no one opened the door too. When the door was finally opened, Peter said "I'm sorry, I came... " he wanted to apologize for coming late, but the Secretary interrupted before he could finish his statement and ushered him to the Board Room. The Secretary said, "I apologize, Peter, for keeping you waiting since 10am. We actually heard when the bell rang at 10am but we were held up in a meeting with our company suppliers.

However, we have sat since 8am to deliberate on your job specification, your office and the salary."

Peter was baffled and said, "Ma'am, I haven't been interviewed yet". The CEO answered him and said, "We decided not to conduct the interview at least to save time and also save the interviewees money on transport. So we looked at the papers for the most appropriate person we wanted and we opted for you. Also, we had tested your patience this morning by keeping you waiting intentionally for 2hrs. That's part of your interview. You won't be disappointed. You'll be shown your office, your secretary and the driver assigned to drive your company's allotted vehicle. You'll be on probation for 2yrs." He got the job!!!

On his way out, his phone rang and it was the wife. She said, "honey, I was delivered of a bouncing baby boy." He immediately named the child 'Miracle' He got a double miracle same day. All the disappointments turned out to favor him. God positioned the mail delivery man to ring the bell at 10am. God also held them up in the meeting until Peter arrived. When you make up your mind to live for God, God will surely favor you in time of need. As long as God is in control, there is hope for all who put their trust on him.

Avoid the use of discriminating words against people of other race. The use of words like 'Niggers' and 'Spics' should be avoided at all cost. It is better to keep silent if you have nothing nice to say to a person or to talk about someone of a different race. Proverbs 17:20 says: "Even fools are considered to be wise when they keep silent." An insane man was once standing near a fence separating a road and the training ground where newly recruited police officers were being trained. The insane man kept watching as the recruits continued their marching training. At the end of their training on that day, one of the training instructors went to the insane man still standing near the fence and asked him saying: "Do you want to join the Police force." The insane man answered and said: "No, am I an insane man to join the police force?" For the insane man, he believed that he was a normal person and felt that it was only people with mental illness would join the police force.

Few months later, as the woman was again leaving for work, one morning, she again asked her husband to watch over her sick old mother living with them. While the woman was at work, the sick old woman died. Her husband, because of the last cat incident, decided not to inform his wife over the phone while she was still at work. At the wife lunch time at work, she called her husband, wanting to know how her sick old mother was doing. Her husband, simply replied her by saying: "Your sick mother has refused to eat." Right from that moment, his wife knew that her sick old mother has died. Jesus said in Matthew 5:37, "Let your yes be yes, and let your no be no."

One good way to avoid discriminating against people of other race is to watch what we say to them or what we say about them. The word of God says in Proverbs 18:21, "The tongue has the power of life and death." What you say to a person can save or destroy that person's life. Again, what you give to a person can save or destroy that person. If you keep giving money to a drug addict, he will keep using the money to buy more drugs until he destroys himself. The story was told about a man who decided to give a beggar a good sum of money, so to turn his life around. He went to the beggar and asked him: "If someone give you $80,000.00, what will you do with it?" The beggar responded that he would die because he has never handle or be given that type of money before. The man then left with his money, and on his way, he met a friend and said to him, "I have just saved a man's life."

Jesus in Matthew 6:24 says "No one can serve two masters; for either he will hate the one and love the other, or he will be devoted to one and despise the other. You cannot be a Christian at the same time be a racist or be lover of social injustice. It is either you are a human being or you are an animal.

A zoology graduate was having difficulties in finding job......

He saw an advert in one of the daily newspaper for a job at a zoo.

At the interview, the manager told him that their gorilla which has been a tourists' attraction has died, so they needed someone to dress and disguise as a gorilla since they have not been able to afford a new gorilla.

The graduate was embarrassed but since the salary was very okay and attractive, he accepted the job offer.

On the first day of his job, he put on the gorilla skin and entered the cage, started jumping up and down, beating his chest while roaring like a gorilla.........

The next day, he put on the gorilla skin and started moving around the zoo again and mistakenly entered another cage until he found himself starring at a lion, the lion roared and started moving towards him. The scared graduate forgot that he was a gorilla and started shouting like a human being "help! help!! help!!!"

The lion leaped onto him, knocked him to the ground and whispered onto one of his ear; Lawrence... it's me Alexander your course mate, no fear, nowhere to find work these days. In fact, you see that crocodile inside that water is Samuel William our course mate.

Many of us must have been victims of racism and social injustice. In the past, when I was offended due to racism or social injustice, I would go on complaining and feeling like a man unjustly stabbed and would not feel solace. I began to feel differently soon after I became a Christian. Now, I know the joy of forgiving my offenders. To a good extent, I no longer see offences as an issue, for as long as we live on this earth, we will be offended. We will also offend others from time to time. Even our very existence is in the hands of God to decide. We did not wake up this morning from our beds because of own abilities or the good functioning of our alarm clocks. Put an alarm clock close to the ears of a dead man, you will discover that he will still remain dead. Read your Bible, you will discover that Jesus Christ and Stephen the deacon, were very quick to forgive those right at the act of killing them. They knew that there is a great reward in forgiveness than in un-forgiveness. If you haven't received Jesus Christ's forgiveness and salvation, may you do so today. If you're already a believer, praise God for what He's done by His great act of love!

We should also learn from a little creature like the ant. In Proverbs 6:8, says: "Go to the ant, you sluggard; consider its ways, and be wise." Many of us hates the ants, we love to kill the ants whenever we see them. The word of God says that we want go o the ants to learn. Sometimes the person God be have divinely brought to help us is the one we want to hate. We may want to hate the person because of his or her color or because of how the look of the person.

On one Sunday morning, a man sat in his balcony enjoying the sunshine and his coffee when a little ant caught his eye; going from one side to the other side of the balcony, carrying a big leaf several times more than its size. The man watched it for more than an hour. He saw that the ant faced many impediments during its journey, paused, took a diversion and then continued towards its destination. At one point the tiny creature came across a crack in the floor. It paused for a little while, analyzed and then laid the huge leaf over the crack, walked over the leaf, picked the leaf on the other side then continued its journey.

The man saw about an hour later that the creature had reached its destination – a tiny hole in the floor which was entrance to its underground dwelling. At this point, the man noticed that the ant was not able to carry the large leaf it carefully managed to its destination into the tiny hole? It simply couldn't! So the tiny creature, after all the painstaking and hard work and exercising great skills, overcoming all the difficulties along the way, just left behind the large leaf and went home empty-handed. The ant had not thought about the end before it began its challenging journey and in the end the large leaf was nothing more than a burden to it. The creature had no option, but to leave it behind, to reach its destination.

The man learned a great lesson that day. Isn't that the truth about our lives? Many of us carry the burden of hating others, the burden of un-forgiveness, the burden of hurt from rejection, the burden of hurt from rape, the burden of hurt of abandonment, the burden of hurt of social in-justice, the burden of hurt of been discriminated against, the burden of wanting to be richer and richer and so on. Just as the ant was unable to carry the leaf into the hole which was it final destination, no Christian will be able carry any of these burden to heaven which will be the Christian's final destination. As long as God is in control, there is hope for all who put their trust on him.

Never allow hate, un-forgiveness and social injustice to destroy you.

A snake entered a Carpentry Shop, and as it crawled to the corner, it went through a saw and hurt itself a little bit. At that time, turned and bit the saw, and biting the saw, it hurt itself badly in the mouth.

Then, not understanding what was happening to it and thinking that the saw was attacking it, it decided to roll around the saw as if wanting to suffocate the saw with it whole body, and shaking with all it strength. It was so, unfortunately, the snake ended up being killed by the saw.

Sometimes we react in anger, thinking about hurting those who hurt us, but we are hurting ourselves. In life, sometimes it is better to ignore situations, people and offenses. Because the consequences can be irreversible and catastrophic.

It is always better to act in love even if it cost a lot, in the face of hate or idle words.

A dog was standing on the edge of a high cliff on a mountain area when a bird few over it, touching it head. The dog in anger, not wanting to let go, jumped up from the cliff to catch to destroy the bird ending smashing its head on the rock below and died. Do not try to take revenge on the evil someone else did to you. We may be hurt by the experience of rejection, abandonment, rape, racism or social injustice. Endeavor to let God, let go. Pursue only what is worth pursuing. The word of God says in Deuteronomy 32:35, that vengeance belongs to

God. Why should you take that which is rightfully belongs to God? To do that, you would be wrongfully rebelling against God, thereby stealing that which belong to God. If a man decides to take vengeance for the wrong done to him, not minding the word of God, he will be like a thief who refuses to acknowledge that he is a thief. A man's character is questionable if he shares the same apartment with a prostitute, always found at un healthy joints, in company of known criminals and everywhere he visits, people complain of things missing. Real Christianity, is to truly practice the teaching of the Bible. This also is the definition of faith. Hope is the confident expectation that things will change to better since there is time for everything. A time to be born and a time to die, a time of social injustice and a time of good social justice.